Life-Changing BIBLE VERSES EVERY WOMAN SHOULD KNOW

Life-Changing
BIBLE VERSES
EVERY WOMAN
SHOULD KNOW

Rebecca Lutzer

HARVEST HOUSE PUBLISHERS
EUGENE, OREGON

Cover design by Dugan Design Group, Bloomington, Minnesota

Cover photo © Dugan Design Group

LIFE-CHANGING BIBLE VERSES EVERY WOMAN SHOULD KNOW
Copyright © 2014 by Rebecca Lutzer
Published by Harvest House Publishers
Eugene, Oregon 97402
www.harvesthousepublishers.com

Library of Congress Cataloging-in-Publication Data
    Lutzer, Rebecca.
    Life-changing Bible verses every woman should know / Rebecca Lutzer.
      pages cm
    ISBN 978-0-7369-5293-4 (pbk.)
    ISBN 978-0-7369-5294-1 (eBook)
    1. Bible—Memorizing. 2. Bible—Quotations. 3. Bible—Indexes. 4. Christian women—Religious life. I. Title.
    BS617.7.L89 2014
    220.07—dc23
                                   2013034394

To all the women in my family and extended family
who have had a part in shaping my life through
the abundant grace of God

Lorisa ~ Lynette ~ Lisa
(daughters)

Mary ~ Julie
(sisters)

June ~ Helen
(aunts)

Patty ~ Janis ~ Danni Lou
(sisters-in-law)

Ruth ~ Esther ~ Jean ~ Charlene
(sisters-in-law)

In loving memory of
Emerald
(mother)

Ada ~ Gertrude
(grandmothers)

Wanda
(mother-in-law)

CONTENTS

Morning Prayer

Let the morning bring me word of your unfailing love,
for I have put my trust in you.
Show me the way I should go,
for to you I entrust my life.
Rescue me from my enemies, LORD,
for I hide myself in you.
Teach me to do your will,
for you are my God;
may your good Spirit
lead me on level ground.
(Psalm 143:8-10 NIV)

Evening Prayer

May my prayer be set before you like incense;
may the lifting up of my hands be like the evening sacrifice.
In peace I will both lie down and sleep;
for you alone, O LORD, make me dwell in safety.
On my bed I remember you;
I think of you through the watches of the night.
Because you are my help,
I sing in the shadow of your wings.
I cling to you;
your right hand upholds me.
(Psalm 141:2 NIV)
(Psalm 4:8)
(Psalm 63:6-8 NIV)

FROM MY HEART TO YOURS

2 Timothy 3:16-17—*All Scripture is breathed out by*
God and profitable for teaching, for reproof, for correction,
and for training in righteousness, that the man [woman]
of God may be complete, equipped for every good work.

God's Word can be trusted above everything else. Circumstances, emotions, health, social norms, morality, the stock market, relationships, the weather—they all change. The Word never changes, but it will change us. It tells us who God is and who we are. It tells us the truth about ourselves, and it is always right. It instructs, convicts, heals, comforts, protects, encourages.

If we will be strong women of faith and conviction, then we must know what we believe and be able to defend it. The best way to do this is to memorize Scripture, to fill our minds and thoughts with truth and instructions that are instantly available in time of need—to keep us from sin, protect us from evil, sustain us in trials, comfort us in sorrow, and give us wisdom and discernment. We can speak the truth in love and bring hope to a broken world.

God gave us His precious Word to teach us how valuable we are to Him, how much He loves us, and how we are to live. Jesus is our example in praying, enduring, forgiving, obeying, loving, resisting temptation, extending grace, being courageous, speaking the truth, and even in dying victoriously. Jesus is our wisdom—the living Word—full of grace and truth.

I wrote this book with the deep conviction that the Bible is the source of our spiritual life, nourishing and sustaining us in a world filled with conflicting voices. Psalm 138:2 tells us that God has exalted (magnified) His Word and His name above all things. My hope and prayer is that every woman who reads this book will develop a desire to memorize God's Word and understand what it teaches.

Join me on this journey as we explore the Scriptures together.

ANGER

Proverbs 19:11 (NIV)—*A person's wisdom yields patience; it is to one's glory to overlook an offense.*

Ephesians 4:26-27—*Be angry and do not sin; do not let the sun go down on your anger, and give no opportunity to the devil.*

James 1:19 (NIV)—*My dear brothers and sisters, take note of this: Everyone should be quick to listen, slow to speak and slow to become angry, because human anger does not produce the righteousness that God desires.*

Anger is a normal and usually healthy human emotion, when it is under control. It can range from a mild irritation to strong feelings of displeasure to intense hostility to destructive rage. In an angry episode, biological changes take place in which the "fight or flight" hormones (adrenaline and noradrenaline) are released, which increases the blood pressure and heart rate. Intense anger can produce a surge of energy that turns into a rage, bypassing the thinking part of the brain and allowing us to say and do things we'll regret later.

Explosive anger can lash out in verbal or physical violence. It can become an effective weapon that can be used to scare other people and make them do what we want. Long-term anger can cause health problems and damage relationships. It will harm and even destroy what is most dear and important in life—family, home, friends, education, career, and even independence and freedom.

There is healthy anger—righteous indignation—that all of us

should have about certain things, such as all kinds of abuse, sex trafficking, rape, murder, abortion, injustice, extortion, addictions, and other criminal and immoral activities. As far as possible, we must do what we can to fight and prevent all forms of evil.

Babies and children do not have to take a course in anger. It is their natural response when their needs and rights are neglected or abused and when they don't get their way or receive the attention they crave. A child usually grows out of temper tantrums, but if this behavior is allowed to become the typical way for that child to react to an experience, they will learn to manipulate people and circumstances with their anger. A child's experience with anger during the first few years of life will greatly affect their future ability to handle anger in an appropriate way.

Why are we so angry? Anger is a normal response to a wrong suffered. There are numerous external causes. A home that produces shame from sexual, physical, emotional, or spiritual abuse. A home where alcoholism, chaos, or dysfunction reign, resulting in fear and communication breakdown. Parenting conflict, rebellious children, unmet needs within marriage, financial problems, accidents, job loss, marital conflict, infidelity, divorce, death of a loved one, disabilities (physical and mental), and shame from failure. These issues often produce people who are easily angered or who lack the ability to control their anger.

Internal causes of anger are also very powerful: self-centered character traits, unrealistic goals, failure in education or business, chronic pain, not enough sleep, perfectionism, poor nutrition, fear, selfishness, feelings of inferiority or rejection, depression and bipolar disorder, lack of confidence or knowledge, sinful behavior, unconfessed sin, and guilt.

Regardless of the cause, anger that is frequent, inappropriate, uncontrolled, and destructive to other people or property must be recognized and addressed. Tiptoeing around an angry person and never confronting them is unhealthy and unwise.

Perhaps you struggle to control your anger. You dislike yourself and regret the many episodes when you have spoken hurtful words, been easily offended, given someone the silent treatment, or even considered how you might punish the offending person. Have you ever mulled over an incident where you were misunderstood, disrespected, neglected, or abused, to the point that you became angry?

It is painful for me to tell you that for several years I was that kind of person. Growing up in an abusive, dysfunctional, shame-based home, I entered marriage with attitudes, memories, and emotions that I hadn't recognized and resolved. As a perfectionist, I was often disappointed by my husband and children, and especially by my own self. I was annoyed when things did not turn out the way I had hoped they would. Many times when I felt misunderstood, disrespected, and mistreated, I reacted to my disappointment and hurt with anger.

I hated being this way. I thought I was hopelessly locked into this kind of reaction and behavior. I felt wretched and often cried out to God to help me and to change me. I was desperate to be different and to be free.

One evening many years ago, I locked my bedroom door and told God that I wasn't leaving until He changed me. Armed with my Bible, a hymnbook, and a notebook, I read the Word, sang hymns, and scribbled down my thoughts. Then I lay prostrate on the floor in the presence of Almighty God. I asked that if I was being influenced by a demon of anger from the evil of my childhood, that He would deliver me. I confessed my sin of anger, asking for forgiveness and cleansing. I wept over the pain of my yesteryears and the pain I had caused my family, and I begged God to release and heal me. My sorrow and the questions about the past that could never be answered, I gave to Jesus.

I left that room different, released from the past and filled with hope, peace, and comfort. I've failed many times since then, but have had the resources to recover, acknowledge my sin, and mature in my response. The old nature with its desire to protect and defend itself will always be with me in this life, but I can choose to react with forgiveness, understanding, and love instead of anger.

The Bible has a great deal to say about anger and what it does to us.

It gives the devil an opportunity to become involved in our lives (Ephesians 4:26-27); it makes us act like a fool (Proverbs 29:11); it makes us disagreeable and quarrelsome (Proverbs 26:21); it leaves us weak spiritually and vulnerable to other sins (Proverbs 25:28); it can lead us to take vengeance into our own hands (Romans 12:17-19); it causes us to be arrogant and rude (1 Corinthians 13:4-5); it does not bring about the righteous life that God desires (James 1:19-20); it can lead to hate and even murder (1 John 3:15).

Many of these Scriptures show us that Satan is actively involved in out-of-control anger. He uses anger to gain a foothold in our lives so that he might destroy us and hurt others. We must resist our enemy through the power of the Scriptures, obedience to God's Word, submission to God, and much prayer.

The Bible also tells us how to overcome ungodly anger. First, *admit that we are angry*. Some people may not realize that their problems are the result of anger. This unacknowledged anger may lie hidden to them after years of emotional numbness and denial. We can give anger many other names or make excuses for our behavior. Counseling may be necessary for some people to uncover the truth.

Second, *receive God's love and acceptance*. Many angry people were brought up in a home that was performance based. Approval and love were given only when a task was done according to expectations. As a child of God, you can rejoice in the sure knowledge of God's unconditional love for those who believe in His Son. Jesus was willing to be forsaken by the Father on the cross so that we would never be forsaken by Him (Romans 8:35-39).

Third, *confess any sin that is hindering us from freedom and fullness in Christ*. Are you covering a hidden sin in your life by being an angry person so that no one can get close to you and find out? We must ask the Holy Spirit to convict us of any activity that is breaking God's laws and forsake anything that we know is morally wrong.

Fourth, *understand Satan's power and plan to destroy us*. When we let the sun go down while we are still angry, we give the devil a foothold in our lives (Ephesians 4:26-27). We are instructed to be self-controlled and alert because the devil is prowling around like a roaring lion looking for someone to devour (1 Peter 5:8-9). We are to resist him by standing firm in our faith. When we submit ourselves to God and His authority, and *then* resist the devil, he will flee from us. As we draw near to God, He draws near to us (James 4:7-8).

Fifth, *we must forgive those who have wronged us.* Unforgiveness creates bitterness, hate, and anger. It robs us of our joy, time, and energy. The person who abused you may have already died, but you continue to be imprisoned by their evil. We can choose to forgive them because God has forgiven us for failing to keep His holy standards (Ephesians 4:32). We must even forgive ourselves. We've all struggled with failure, personal disappointment, guilt, and sorrow from our own sin. It is arrogant for us to think we cannot forgive others and ourselves when Christ has forgiven us.

Sixth, *recognize God's sovereignty in our life.* Without explanation, God allows trials, sorrows, difficult circumstances, and even evil to be a part of our lives. His many purposes may be unknown to us, but His ultimate purpose is to refine us and make us more like Jesus. He takes the pain and suffering of those who love Him and makes them work together for their good (Romans 8:28-29).

Seventh, *God gives us the ability to control our anger.* As believers, we have the power of the Holy Spirit within to enable us to have victory over the desires of our bodies, minds, and emotions. We can ask for help whenever we need it. The fruit of the Spirit is love, joy, peace, patience, kindness, goodness, faithfulness, gentleness, and *self-control* (Galatians 5:16-26).

Eighth, *we are to give thanks in all circumstances.* As beloved daughters of Jesus Christ, the challenging, grueling, and incomprehensible circumstances of our lives are part of His will for us (1 Thessalonians 5:18). When we stop arguing with God and, in submission, accept His will, our anger will dissipate. And then, dear one, He is free to work all things together for our good. Trust Him!

Taking God's Word to Heart

1. Look up every Scripture verse listed in this chapter and write down what the Holy Spirit reveals to you about your anger.

2. What things make you angry, and how have you learned to control your anger in a biblical way?

3. If you're struggling to control your anger, what have you learned that will help you?

4. Spend an hour in God's presence asking Him to reveal anything in your past or in the present that is causing you to be angry. Confess all sin, and choose to forgive those who have wronged you. Begin the journey to healing and wholeness.

APPEARANCE

1 Samuel 16:7 (NIV)—*"The LORD does not look at the things people look at. People look at the outward appearance, but the LORD looks at the heart."*

Proverbs 31:30—*Charm is deceitful, and beauty is vain, but a woman who fears the LORD is to be praised.*

1 Peter 3:3-4—*Do not let your adorning be external—the braiding of hair and the putting on of gold jewelry, or the clothing you wear—but let your adorning be the hidden person of the heart with the imperishable beauty of a quiet spirit, which in God's sight is very precious.*

Every woman wants to be beautiful—and thin. Equally as strong is the need to be desired and wanted. God made us that way. It is part of the feminine mystique. History is filled with stories of men vying for the most beautiful women, and of women going to great lengths to be the most attractive and desirable. This behavior has brought down kings and men in high places. Women of class and in a higher economic status have sometimes been bypassed for the beautiful peasant girl, such as Cinderella. These are accounts of intrigue, slander, lying, and even murder. The competition is fierce. It may be true to say that physical beauty ranks the highest on a list of what women want most.

What is the relationship between beauty and happiness? How attractive do you have to be before you can accept and feel good about yourself? Will you have to live with sadness and emotional pain if you are not really pretty and look rather ordinary? Worse yet, what can you expect if you are born with a physical defect or disability?

Our culture answers these questions decisively. You had better be attractive if you want to be successful in your career or find the most eligible bachelor to marry. If you are unfortunate enough to have been born without the gift of beauty, you'd better do something about it or you will go unnoticed and suffer rejection. It's not who you *are*, but how you *look* that matters.

"No one cared about my good grades and any of my achievements until I got implants," one woman told me. "Now I'm noticed by men and feel valuable. I knew I could never be happy unless I was beautiful."

Beauty is synonymous with looking sexy and being desirable. Customizing the body is a multibillion dollar business, and it's not just for the rich and famous. Women know that men can see better than they can think. This puts an unbearable burden on young girls and women to go to any length to look sexy and be noticed.

Who is to blame for this obsession with physical appearance? Hollywood and the fashion industry magnify this false standard. Movies, soap operas, and beauty pageants feature the perfect and beautiful people of the world, those who were born with a wonderful confluence of genes and those who achieve perfection by severe dieting, excessive exercise, and plastic surgery. As psychologist James Dobson wrote, "We reserve our praise and admiration for a select few who have been blessed at birth with the characteristics we value most highly."

However, there is a negative side to being beautiful. Even the beautiful people have misgivings and self-doubt when they look into the mirror. Attractive young women are sought out and exploited by men to satisfy their sexual cravings. It's not too strong to say that beauty can be a curse. Marilyn Monroe revealed in private papers that despite her relationships with many famous men, she never felt loved and valued.

Beauty is overrated. It can lead to loneliness, alcohol and drug abuse, and suicide.

We belong to God by reason of creation—that is the starting point for a scriptural view of the body.

> So God created man in his own image,
>   in the image of God he created him;
>   male and female he created them.
>   (Genesis 1:27)

The first human beings were created with a spirit so that they could communicate with God. Every person who has ever been born has been created in the image of God.

Self-acceptance—that is, accepting ourselves as God created us—lies at the heart of our sense of well-being and spiritual development. The foundation of self-acceptance is the knowledge that we were created by God and formed according to His design in our mothers' wombs. When we read the words of Psalm 139:13-16, there is no doubt that God regards a fetus as a baby. And Isaiah the prophet wrote,

> "This is what the LORD says—
>   your Redeemer, who formed you in the womb."
>   (Isaiah 44:24 NIV)

Isaiah also affirmed that God spoke to him before his birth:

> Before I was born the LORD called me;
>   from my mother's womb he has spoken my name.
>   (49:1 NIV)

The implications of God's direct involvement in our formation as a developing fetus are important for us to understand.

First, through the gene pool of our parents and ancestors, God determines our height, body shape, skin color, facial features, and the color of our eyes and hair.

Second, God chooses our gender. He determines whether we will be a man or a woman. Based on what we have just read in Scripture, there is no doubt that sex-change operations are an attack against the image of God formed in every human being. It is He who created us "male and female"; thus to change from one gender to another is a form of rebellion against the Creator. It is defiance to believe that the Almighty made a mistake when men were created as men and women as women.

Finally, God determines our limitations, defects, and deformities. When God told Moses to lead the Israelites out of Egypt, Moses complained because he did not have the gift of speech (possibly an impediment). And God declared, "Who gave human beings their mouths? Who makes them deaf or mute? Who gives them sight or makes them blind? Is it not I, the LORD?" (Exodus 4:11 NIV). Those whom others turn away from, God is pleased to honor and use for His glory.

We've all wondered where God was when we were put together. We're either too tall or too short; breasts too small or too big; hair too curly or too straight; nose, ears, or feet not quite the way we'd like them. We'll know God in a deeper way when we can look in the mirror and acknowledge His sovereignty and accept our appearance with gratitude as from the hand of our wise and loving Creator.

> "Woe to those who quarrel with their Maker,
>   those who are nothing but potsherds
>   among the potsherds on the ground.
> Does the clay say to the potter,
>   'What are you making?'"
>   (Isaiah 45:9 NIV)

We also belong to God by reason of *redemption*. Many people think, *It's my body, so I have the right to do with it whatever I want.* The Bible tells us something different: "Do you not know that your body is a temple of the Holy Spirit within you, whom you have from God? You are not your own, for you were bought with a price. So glorify God in your body" (1 Corinthians 6:19-20). Our bodies should be covered with modest clothing so that we can be an effective witness for Christ (2 Timothy 2:9-10). We can teach our daughters that their character and inner beauty are far more important than their outer beauty.

Cosmetic surgery is not inherently sinful. Deformed children often benefit from special operations to improve their features and their health, such as those with a cleft palate. Some women need breast reduction surgery to ease back pain. Obese people who lose a lot of weight need surgery to remove flabby skin and fat. Aging brings about unsightly changes that can be adjusted, such as drooping eyelids that can affect vision. We can understand alterations made to improve one's appearance, but we cannot condone plastic surgeries done to make a woman sexually provocative.

God created our bodies as a vessel for His attributes, such as love, joy, and peace. He wants to use our bodies as the means to a greater end—the formation of Christian character and the spread of the gospel to the ends of the earth. We are His hands, feet, eyes, and ears. A body that is the temple of the Holy Spirit is a holy place in which God dwells. This is why Paul taught that the body itself did not have to look good in order for the treasure within it to shine forth. "But we have this treasure in jars of clay to show that this all-surpassing power is from God and not from us" (2 Corinthians 4:7).

For centuries people have wondered what Jesus looked like. Artists have tried to paint Him based on the knowledge of Middle Eastern culture and their own imaginations. A clue about the appearance of Jesus is given by the prophet Isaiah:

> He had no beauty or majesty to attract us to him,
>> nothing in his appearance that we should desire him.
>> (53:2 NIV)

From this description, we may conclude that Jesus was not a handsome man. There is no reference to His physical features in the New Testament. Again, we turn to Isaiah and read that His body was so badly disfigured by His accusers prior to His crucifixion that it was "marred beyond human likeness" (52:14 NIV).

God the Son stepped out of heaven to become human so that He could die as the God-man to redeem the fallen human race. What mattered most to Him was not His appearance but doing His Father's will. Jesus used His ordinary body to perform many miracles as documented in the Gospels. He taught the religious leaders and the common people about who He was and about their needy spiritual condition. He forgave sins and healed many, and then He died on the cross to provide our salvation.

Jesus stands as a powerful rebuke to the body worship of our generation. He invites all who would follow Him to adopt a higher set of values, to look beyond the physical to the eternal, and to learn to accept ourselves and others, not for how we look, but for who we are in Christ.

Beloved women, you are beautiful!

Taking God's Word to Heart

1. What have you learned about God's purpose in creating you?

2. Why is it so difficult for us to accept ourselves for who we are? How attractive do you have to be before you accept and feel good about yourself?

3. How does understanding who you are in Christ enable you to accept yourself as God created you?

4. What does Jesus's life teach you about appearance and accepting yourself?

THE ARMOR OF GOD

Ephesians 6:10-12—*Finally, be strong in the Lord and in the strength of his might. Put on the whole armor of God, that you may be able to stand against the schemes of the devil. For we do not wrestle against flesh and blood, but against the rulers, against the authorities, against the cosmic powers over this present darkness, against the spiritual forces of evil in the heavenly places.*

1 Peter 5:8-9 (NIV)—*Be alert and of sober mind. Your enemy the devil prowls around like a roaring lion looking for someone to devour. Resist him, standing firm in the faith, because you know that the family of believers throughout the world is undergoing the same kind of sufferings.*

Revelation 12:11— *"And they have conquered him by the blood of the Lamb and by the word of their testimony, for they loved not their lives even unto death."*

If our eyes were opened to see the invisible world, we would be surprised at the amount of activity around us. We would also be surprised that Satan (also called the devil in Scripture) and his demons are actively involved in so many of our temptations, struggles, and desires to sin. This reminder comes to us from the apostle Paul, who surely knew what it was like to be harassed and opposed by the spiritual forces of darkness: "we wanted to come to you—I, Paul, again and again—but Satan hindered us" (1 Thessalonians 2:18).

C.S. Lewis warned that there are two mistakes we can make when we think of Satan. The first is to ignore or even disregard him; many today do not believe the devil is real. The second mistake is to be obsessed with him, giving the devil more attention than he deserves or ascribing to him greater power than he has. We must guard against both extremes.

Jesus forced demons to acknowledge who He was before He cast them out. They knew exactly who He was. He had absolute authority over the spirit world. Jesus's death on the cross gives us authority over Satan and his world of evil and darkness.

Before we talk about putting on the armor of God to withstand Satan's deceptions and power, we must realize that he is actively involved in matters that we face every day. The devil tempted Jesus with the lust of the flesh, the lust of the eyes, and the pride of life. And he tempts us with the same means—to be immoral (1 Corinthians 7:1-5); to deny the Lord (as he did with Simon Peter); to be dishonest; to be caught up in the doctrines of false prophets (2 Corinthians 11:1-6); to worship people, money, fame, and power; to neglect prayer and reading and studying the Bible; to fill our time with technology and our minds with ungodly images on TV and the Internet; to influence and control our emotions (Ephesians 4:25-27).

I have no doubt that he uses all of the above tactics to try to destroy marriages, our children, relationships, and even churches. Satan lies to us, deceives us, blinds us to truth, binds us to certain sins, torments us, uses us, and tries to separate us from God. He would destroy us but for God's grace and protection.

It is important to keep in mind that Satan is a created spirit being and that he cannot act independently of God (Job 1 and Luke 22:31-34). God uses Satan to discipline the disobedient (1 Samuel 18:10), to test the obedient (Matthew 4:1-11), to keep us from sinning (2 Corinthians 12:9), and to purify the righteous (Job 1–2). He can be in only one place at one time; he cannot be in both Chicago and Cairo simultaneously. Satan has thousands of minions, evil spirits under his authority who are sent to inflict, tempt, oppress, harass, and deceive and to separate us from fellowship with God, as he did with Adam and Eve (Genesis 2:1-7). Evil spirits attempt to make sin look attractive, fun, and harmless so that we will not fear it and run from it. That is why we must be prepared to withstand the schemes and the deceptions of the devil.

What is the armor of God? Paul visualizes a Roman soldier dressed for hand-to-hand combat, and he uses the soldier's armor as an analogy of how we should be dressed to face our spiritual enemy. Paul lists six pieces of armor we should wear to "be able to withstand in the evil day, and having done all, to stand firm" (Ephesians 6:13)—the belt of truth, the breastplate of righteousness, the shoes of the gospel of peace, the shield of faith, the helmet of salvation, and the sword of the Spirit, which is the Word of God (6:14-17).

Space forbids a detailed description of each piece, but a brief explanation of Paul's instruction and how to apply it is important.

First and foremost, these pieces of armor represent a lifestyle. They represent habits and values that we treasure in our personal commitment to holy living. The best way to put on the *belt of truth* is to accept Christ as "the way and the truth and the life" (John 14:6), and then live a life characterized by truthfulness (demons are liars who want us also to become deceptive [John 8:44]). We put on the *breastplate of righteousness* by receiving the gift of Christ's righteousness (2 Corinthians 5:21), and then we must live a life characterized by righteousness. We put on the shoes of the *gospel of peace* by living out the gospel and sharing it with others. We put on the *shield of faith* by believing and trusting God's Word and promises (Hebrews 11:6; 2 Peter 1:4). We put on the *helmet of salvation* by filling our minds with the theology of God's redemption and victory on the cross, which protects our thoughts and brings them into captivity (2 Corinthians 10:5). And finally, we take in our hands our weapon—the *sword of the Spirit*, which is the Word of God (Matthew 4:1-7).

Once we have put on the armor of God, it is a daily process to make sure it's in place and functioning properly—that we are "fully clothed" to do battle with our enemy. We must be vigilant that all repairs are made to ensure there's no entry point that could give our enemy an advantage. Knowing the wiles of the devil, we must be careful not to put ourselves in situations where we know we will be tempted. We will not be careless about where we go and the people we spend time with. To summarize, we do not go into the devil's territory with the assumption that we can return unharmed and whenever we wish.

Second, Paul concludes his description of the armor with these words, "praying at all times in the Spirit, with all prayer and supplication. To that end keep alert with all perseverance, making supplication for all the saints" (Ephesians 6:18). In other words, the armor must be "well oiled" with persistent prayer. This means we must be praying constantly—in an attitude of prayer for ourselves and others—because Satan and his evil spirits seek our destruction. They want us to make a disastrous decision that will determine the direction of our lives for years to come. Satan will offer us a million dollars today, but he will take something from us that can never be restored. With Christ's help we can find our way back, but critical damage may have been done to ourselves, to others, and to the whole family of God. It never pays to serve Satan.

We must be alert, sober-minded, and watchful because our "enemy the devil prowls around like a roaring lion looking for someone to devour. Resist him, standing firm in the faith, because you know that the family of believers throughout the world is undergoing the same kind of sufferings" (1 Peter 5:8-9 NIV). Satan wants to do the same thing to us that he did to Adam and Eve—cut off our fellowship with God, and he never tires, never gives up, and never bypasses an opportunity. Vigilance is crucial.

Finally, and most importantly, we must never forget that Christ's death and resurrection was a fatal blow to Satan, who is proud to be "the god of this world." Jesus overcame the deepest, darkest, strongest evil that Satan can ever marshal. Paul wrote, "He disarmed the rulers and authorities and put them to open shame, by triumphing over them in him" (Colossians 2:15). Today, Satan is out on bail, but his sentence has been pronounced and his doom assured. This means that we fight against him and his assistants with confidence that our victory over him has been purchased by Christ's hard-won victory. We stand against him with strength not weakness, with courage not fear. We can participate in the triumph of Jesus with faith, by which, Paul says, we can "extinguish all the flaming darts of the evil one" (Ephesians 6:16).

As children of God, we have been completely delivered from Satan's kingdom into God's kingdom through faith in the atoning blood of the Lord Jesus Christ (Colossians 1:13), and God relates to those in His kingdom as a loving father to precious children (Romans 8:15). When we clothe ourselves in the spiritual armor and use the authority God has granted us in the spiritual realm, we can boldly command the obedience of Satan's forces in the powerful name of the Lord Jesus Christ (Matthew 4:10; Mark 8:33). We need never cower before them. We have the means to be totally victorious over them—*if* we keep ourselves spiritually vigilant to recognize their attacks. [1]

Taking God's Word to Heart

1. What is the armor of God?

2. Why is it important to every Christian and how do we use it?

3. What piece of armor do you need the most? Where are you the most vulnerable to the devil's temptations and schemes?

BECOMING A WOMAN OF GRACE

2 Corinthians 2:14—*But thanks be to God, who in Christ always leads us in triumphal procession, and through us spreads the fragrance of the knowledge of him everywhere. For we are the aroma of Christ to God among those who are being saved and among those who are perishing.*

1 Peter 5:10—*And after you have suffered a little while, the God of all grace, who has called you to his eternal glory in Christ, will himself restore, confirm, strengthen, and establish you.*

2 Peter 3:18—*But grow in the grace and knowledge of our Lord and Savior Jesus Christ. To him be the glory both now and to the day of eternity. Amen.*

A gracious woman is poised and polite, kind, tactful, and deferring to others. Even when we achieve these human graces, our true nature can still come through, and underneath we can be cynical, bitter about life's difficulties, angry, and self-centered. Being a Christian does not inoculate us from these natural tendencies, but it means that we have the Holy Spirit who enables us to confess them as sin and have victory over them. We are instructed to "grow in grace and knowledge of our Lord and Savior Jesus Christ" (2 Peter 3:18).

These are the graces of a mature Christian woman: moral purity, humility, honesty, wisdom, and a life that produces the fruit of the Spirit, which is love, joy, peace, patience, kindness, goodness, faithfulness, gentleness, and self-control. Essentially, it is being able to say no to fleshly and worldly passions and to live in control of our emotions and body. This is possible because Jesus Christ gave Himself to redeem us from all wickedness and to purify us for Himself (Titus 2:11-14). God's grace changes us and enables us to live as godly women in a sinful world.

Growing in grace is a long, hard process. It does not take place quickly or easily. It is a lifelong journey. Sometimes the path is steep and rocky. Sometimes we stumble, fall, and get injured. Sometimes the path is obscured by thick brush and thorns. Sometimes we get sick or become weary. God's Word lights our path and shows us the way:

> Your word is a lamp to my feet
>   and a light for my path.
> (Psalm 119:105)

We cannot make the journey without it as our light and guide.

Growing in grace involves pain and suffering. There are no options here. Each of us will experience physical, emotional, and spiritual suffering many times during our pilgrimage. Often, God gives us no explanation for our suffering. Elisabeth Elliot says that suffering is one of two things: not having something you want, or having something you don't want. Very simple and yet profound.

Think of a young *married* woman who is infertile and longing for a baby to hold in her arms. On the other hand, think of the young *unmarried* woman who finds herself pregnant and longing to get rid of her baby. One woman desperately longs to be pregnant; the other woman desperately longs not to be. Both are suffering. Consider the *single* woman, longing for love and a husband, and the unhappily *married* woman who longs to be free again. Each wants what the other has.

Many things hinder God's grace and our growth. Our bodies are filled with urgent needs, and our minds are filled with endless longings. These needs and longings are demanding. Sometimes our hormones rage and our fleshly senses control us. Sometimes our hopes and unfulfilled dreams overwhelm us, and we choose to step out of God's waiting room and meet our needs in an ungodly way.

What have you longed for and not received? What have you received that you have not longed for?

We can see how some of our suffering comes when we think that God is too slow, and in our desperation we decide to take matters into our own hands. We fear that He may never give us what we long for, and we doubt His love and goodness. Our needs and longings are not wrong—God made us this way. But when we choose to meet our needs and fulfill our longings outside of God's will, we usually suffer painful and long-lasting consequences.

When our petitions turn to whining, our disappointments to anger, and our tears to demands, we are sinning.

Most women long to be married—to have the love of a man, a home and security, and children. They pray earnestly and wait patiently for God to send their handsome prince. But when their prayers go unanswered and their patience wears thin, many a woman has married a man she knew deep in her heart she should not marry. Perhaps he was unsaved or she saw something in his life and character that was questionable, warning her not to marry him. Even though God was saying no, she was willing to take a chance and compromise, thinking she could live with the consequences or that this man would change after marriage.

Oh, how deceived we are to think like this. Apart from a miracle of God, people seldom change for the better. Some men, even Christian men, are set in their ways and patterns of sinful behavior, and sometimes after marriage they become overtly or deceptively evil. We cannot underestimate the sorrows and difficulties that will come to us when we step outside of God's will and protection.

There is a danger that we take advantage of grace. Jude, the Lord's half brother, spoke about those who "pervert the grace of God into sensuality and deny our only Master and Lord, Jesus Christ" (Jude 4). And the apostle Paul warned his readers, "Are we to continue in sin that grace may abound? By no means! How can we who died to sin still live in it?" (Romans 6:1-3).

We may think, *If I sin, I know that God will forgive me, so it's safe to sin.* This is perverse and dangerous reasoning because it means that we will come under God's discipline. God loves us too much to let us flout His grace (Hebrews 12:5-6). In fact, if we sin without receiving God's discipline, it might well be that we are not His children.

When the lonely, unhappy *single* woman seeks love and companionship outside of marriage, she will suffer. And when the lonely, unhappy *married* woman seeks love and companionship outside of her marriage, she too will suffer. God uses the consequences of our sin to discipline, change, and purify us.

Sometimes our suffering becomes almost unbearable before we are willing to submit to God's sovereignty. When we return to our heavenly Father in repentance and submission, it will allow His grace to once again flow in our lives, for "where sin increased, grace abounded all the more" (Romans 5:20). God's grace will come to help us in our suffering and give us wisdom to know what to do in difficult, desperate circumstances, even situations caused by our sin, if we are willing to confess and forsake it. The promise in Hebrews 4:16 is infinitely valuable, "Let us then with confidence draw near to the throne of grace, that we may receive mercy and find grace to help in time of need."

It may appear that I am overusing Scripture, but since we know that God loves and honors His Word, where else should we go to find truth that will sustain and carry us through the hard times in our lives? Romans 8:28 is a classic and cannot be overemphasized, "And we know that for those who love God all things work together for good, for those who are called according to his purpose." God has proved the truth of this verse over and over again in my life, and I trust in yours too.

How should we as women growing in grace respond when God doesn't give us what we want and ask for? Instead of whining or developing sinful attitudes and habits, we can entrust ourselves into His wise, loving care. When answers to our prayers are delayed or denied, it is so that more might be given and more received. *The work that God does in us while we wait is more important than the thing we wait for.* God is always working to accomplish His will in our lives even when we cannot detect what He is doing.

Have we considered that what we think is good for us might not be? At times I have prayed for things that I thought I needed or that would make me happy. But when they finally arrived, they became a burden or brought bitterness. Are we willing to wait so that God can bring about His plan and give us the very best? In Bible college I taped this excellent advice on the wall of my room: "God gives the best to those who leave the choice with Him."

Sometimes God is doing His work in another person through our waiting and our suffering. That may be hard to accept, but God's ways and purposes are so different from ours. I often quote Romans 11:33 to remind myself that God is in charge and I'm not: "Oh, the depth of the riches both of the wisdom and knowledge of God! How unsearchable are His judgments and His ways past finding out!" (NKJV). We must surrender our wills to God and ask Him to give us what He wants us to have.

As we wait, watch, suffer, learn, and grow, we begin to ask God how we can fit into His plan and serve Him rather than ourselves. We begin to see that we exist to serve God, not that He exists to serve us and our selfish desires. Our prayers change, and our focus shifts to how we can glorify God. It's no longer, *God, please fix it or change it.* Most often God doesn't change our circumstances, but He changes us within our circumstances. Our prayer becomes, *How can my life bring glory and pleasure to you, God?* We go from being self-centered to being God-centered. We plead with God to give us what *He* wants so that we can give it back to Him.

Every life situation provides us an opportunity to become a woman of grace. We now understand that the suffering, disappointments, and injustices of life come to us through the loving providence of God. One of my favorite verses is 1 Peter 5:10:

And after you have suffered a little while, the God of all grace, who has called you to his eternal glory in Christ, will himself restore, confirm, strengthen, and establish you.

Beloved women, do you think that suffering is unfair and overrated and that God just doesn't want you to have any fun? That the difficult and painful things in your life have no meaning except to make you miserable? Please read that verse again...and again. This promise makes our suffering worthwhile as we become women of grace. Restored. Confirmed. Strengthened. Established.

Taking God's Word to Heart

1. What does growing in grace mean?

2. Is anything hindering you from growing in grace that you haven't surrendered to God?

3. What things are you doing to become a woman of grace?

4. Are you more mature today than you were five years ago? In what ways?

COURAGE

Joshua 1:9—*"Have not I commanded you? Be strong and courageous. Do not be frightened and do not be dismayed, for the Lord your God is with you wherever you go."*

Psalm 31:24—*Be strong, and let your heart take courage, all you who wait for the LORD!*

Courage and character are closely linked. Who we are inside and what we believe will guide us to make either wise or unwise decisions. Who we think we are is not as important as *what* we think, because what we think, *we are.* Character is more than behaving properly at the right time; it's doing the right thing when no one is there to observe us.

Courage takes it one more step: It's doing the right thing even when we're tempted to do the wrong thing. It's standing up for what we know is right even when it goes against peer pressure and our narcissistic, decadent culture. It is living by our personal honor and integrity. Courage is the God-given ability to do what we should, no matter the cost or consequences.

What does courage look like in the lives of women today?

- Ending any relationship or friendship that entices me to sin

- Resigning from a job that requires me to do anything illegal or immoral

- Turning off television shows that portray immorality and obscenity
- Getting rid of all reading material that is sexually explicit in word and picture
- Having deeply held beliefs based on God's Word that will help me make good decisions
- Taking the time to teach my children who God is and how He wants us to live to obey and please Him
- Standing for righteousness even if it means I'll be ridiculed, misjudged, or fired
- Telling the truth even when I feel embarrassed, rejected, or that it may cost me
- Doing the best thing for my family even though I may have to sacrifice some of my needs and wants

Have you had the experience of knowing what you should do, but you turned away because of fear? All of us fear the risks of embarking on a path whose destination is uncertain. Standing up for your convictions in today's culture and working environments is challenging, perhaps even dangerous. Just how far should we go to stand alone for righteousness? How do we exercise such courage?

First of all, *we must build relationships with people* in our work or school environment. Often we discover that people are much more open-minded when we take an interest in their lives and their personal challenges. Arguments, conflicts, and the reinforcing of battle lines take place when we don't make the effort to build bridges of friendship with those we disagree with.

Second, when we do take a courageous stand against political correctness or the expectations of our culture, or the laws that restrict our religious freedom, *we must do so with respect and grace.* Most important, we must explain to others why we feel so deeply about our convictions. The New Testament makes it clear that every predicament in which we find ourselves within the world is another opportunity to represent Christ.

Third, when we are unsure what our response should be in a particular situation, *we must ask God for wisdom* to know how we should conduct ourselves (James 1:5-6). He will help us to discern when we should speak and when we should remain silent, when we should submit to the law or cultural expectations and when we should exercise our God-given courage and refuse to go along with questionable practices and limitations forced upon us.

We often stand in need of a promise that, if we do what we know is right, God will help us, no matter the cost. Moses's successor, Joshua, is a case study in courage. He needed reassurance and support from God as he prepared to lead the nation of Israel into the promised land of Canaan.

Forty years earlier, twelve spies had entered the land, and when they returned, only two of them—Joshua and Caleb—encouraged the people to keep moving forward, trusting God for victory. The majority turned back in fear when they learned there were giants in the land. Because they lacked courage, they backed away from a wonderful opportunity to prove that God was greater than the obstacles they faced.

Now, with that unbelieving group of people dead, God did not want Joshua to repeat the same mistake the previous generation had made. Only a courageous leader could take a fearful people and lead them to victory against formidable odds.

Joshua and his people needed an incredible dose of courage. They needed the assurance that they were not alone and that there were benefits to stepping out in faith and following God's plan for them. God had said He would take up their cause and fight for them, but how could they be sure? Here are the words of God to Joshua:

> "No man shall be able to stand before you all the days of
> your life. Just as I was with Moses, so I will be with you. I
> will not leave you or forsake you. Be strong and courageous,

for you shall cause this people to inherit the land that I swore to their fathers to give them. Only be strong and very courageous, being careful to do according to all the law that Moses my servant commanded you. Do not turn from it to the right hand or to the left, that you may have good success wherever you go. *This Book of the Law shall not depart from your mouth, but you shall meditate on it day and night, so that you may be careful to do according to all that is written in it. For then you will make your way prosperous, and then you will have good success.* Have I not commanded you? Be strong and courageous. Do not be frightened, and do not be dismayed, for the LORD your God is with you wherever you go" (Joshua 1:5-9).

In context, the promise given to Joshua was entwined with the command to "meditate on [the law of God] day and night." This focus would achieve two objectives: (1) his mind would be filled with faith toward God, and (2) it would keep him from being distracted with lesser things. God expressly told Joshua should not turn from the law "to the right hand or to the left." Joshua he would have to remember that God was bigger than the giants and stronger than fortified armies.

Here we have the secret of our own courage in the midst of trial and danger. Joshua was to speak the Word of God—it was not to depart from his mouth. As he obediently did what the Lord commanded, faith arose in his heart and success and blessing followed. Even so, we must memorize the promises of God so that we can speak them, not just to ourselves but back to God. This replaces fear so that we, like Joshua, can be courageous and take reasonable risks in the strength of the Lord.

Joshua knew that the voice he listened to would determine the direction he would walk. If he listened to his emotions, he would remain content in the desert. If he could hear the whispers of his enemies, he would be intimidated and fearful. If he heard the criticism of the people, he would be distracted and weak. Only if he regularly heard the voice of God would he have the courage to do what was impossible.

Recently I heard of a woman who works for an employer who berates her at every opportunity. Every day this committed Christian has to listen to false accusations and criticism. She fears going to work in such a hostile environment. But she has learned to prepare for each day by arising early to fill her heart and mind with God's Word. This gives her the courage to endure verbal abuse for another day.

After all, the harshest thing that could happen to us is some form of suffering—the worst being death. And yet Jesus reminds us that even then we need not fear those who are able to kill the body but not the soul, but rather fear those who are able to destroy both the body and soul in hell (Matthew 10:28). Courage even in the face of impending death has marked the lives of the martyrs who have gone before us.

The virtue of courage also enables us to witness for Christ. Dr. Harry Ironside, who pastored the Moody Church in Chicago during the 1940s, said that as a boy he wanted to receive Christ as Savior, but he told his mother, "All the boys will laugh at me." And his mother wisely replied, "Harry, they may laugh you into hell, but they can never laugh you out of it."

Courageous Christians cannot always follow the path of least resistance; sometimes they must say no to comfort and safety and take risks. During recent persecutions in Egypt, Christian youth took to the streets of Cairo wearing T-shirts with the slogan, "Martyr by Request." They were responding to the violence against Christians—the raiding of homes and the burning of churches.

Their courage should inspire us to stand for truth and righteousness even at great personal cost. Whether it is in a small matter or a more serious one, God will give us the courage to stand up for our convictions and leave the consequences with Him.

Taking God's Word to Heart

1. In what ways have you had to exercise courage as a Christian?

2. When have you failed to be courageous?

3. What does Joshua 1:5-9 teach us to do that will build up and maintain our courage?

4. In light of what we have learned, what important action or decision do you need to make that will take courage?

DISCIPLINE OF GOD [2]

Hebrews 12:6-7,10-11 (NIV)—*"The Lord disciplines
the one he loves, and he chastens everyone he accepts
as his son." Endure hardship as discipline; God is
treating you as his children. For what children are not
disciplined by their father?...But God disciplines us for
our good, in order that we may share in his holiness. No
discipline seems pleasant at the time, but painful. Later
on, however, it produces a harvest of righteousness
and peace for those who have been trained by it.*

Psalm 119:67,71—*Before I was afflicted I went astray,
but now I keep your word...
It is good for me that I was afflicted,
that I might learn your statutes.*

Revelation 3:19—*"Those whom I love, I reprove
and discipline, so be zealous and repent."*

No one enjoys discipline. It hurts, and it can be messy and embarrassing. We discipline our children because they need it, they learn the value and benefits of obedience, and it helps decrease their desire to sin.

One of the most important responsibilities a father has is to discipline his children. A father who does not take this assignment seriously does not understand the power, purpose, and value of discipline. The writer of the book of Hebrews tells us, "'The Lord disciplines the one he loves, and he chastens everyone he accepts as his son.' Endure hardship as discipline; God is treating you as his children. For what children are not disciplined by their father?" (Hebrews 12:6-7 NIV). The basis of discipline is that God is our Father. Every one of God's sons and daughters receives discipline; indeed, it is proof that we are His children.

Discipline is the correcting work of God in our lives, and it comes from His great love for us through trials and the consequences of sin. It is designed to change, protect, and restore us.[3] In this age of grace and in our American way of thinking, God should prove His love by delivering us from the hardships of life. But we need to understand that it is out of His love, wisdom, and knowledge that He disciplines us for our correction and training. He does not discipline us arbitrarily.

> Blessed is the one you discipline, LORD,
>   the one you teach from your law;
> you grant them relief from days of trouble.
>   (Psalms 94:12-13 NIV)

The most important purpose of divine discipline is to force us to seek a deeper relationship with God. Pain produces obedience and holiness: "but he disciplines us for our good, that we may share his holiness" (Hebrews 12:10); and,

> O LORD, in distress they sought you;
>   they poured out a whispered prayer
>   when your discipline was upon them.
>   (Isaiah 26:16)

Satan's deception is that we can live our lives independently of God. He doesn't care if we believe in God or fill our schedules with a lot of spiritual activities—as long as he can get us to run on our own steam rather than living in conscious dependence on the power of the Holy Spirit.[4]

The first prerequisite for holiness is *submission*. Every time we were disciplined as children, we could either rebel or yield to our father's hand. The discipline either softened us or made us more rebellious.

God may frequently increase the amount of pain to bring us to the place of complete yieldedness and dependence.

The second prerequisite for holiness is *loyalty*. Almost every trial of life forces us to choose between loyalty to ourselves or loyalty to God. Will we cling to what we love and desire or will we give everything to God to do with as He knows best? Abraham's loyalty was severely tested when God asked him to sacrifice his son Isaac. Generations to come have stood in awe of what a man was willing to do for God. God may test us in a similar way, asking that we open our hands and give to Him what is most precious to us.

The third prerequisite for holiness is to *fear sin*. As the psalmist says,

> Before I was afflicted I went astray,
> > but now I keep your word.
> > > (Psalm 119:67)

Those of us who have been to God's woodshed and felt the pain of our disobedience are not inclined to repeat our sin. The punishment hurts for a time, "but later it yields the peaceful fruit of righteousness to those who have been trained by it" (Hebrews 12:11).

How can we know the difference between God testing us to produce holiness and God disciplining us for our disobedience? We may not always be able to detect the relationship between sin and its consequences. We often interpret our tragedies in light of our past sins, but the calamities of life, such as sickness or natural disasters, are not necessarily a judgment for specific sins and failures. Sometimes the consequences of our words and actions become the discipline.

Sometimes God allows Satan to be involved in both our testing and discipline. Two of the most godly men who ever lived, Job and the apostle Paul, are stunning examples of Satan's direct involvement in their suffering.

> And the LORD said to Satan, "Have you considered my
> servant Job, that there is none like him on the earth, a

blameless and upright man, who fears God and turns away
from evil?…Behold, all that he has is in your hand. Only
against him do not stretch out your hand" (Job 1:8,12).

Paul was called by the will of God to be an apostle of Jesus Christ
and to bear in his body the sufferings of Christ (Galatians 6:17). He
had been given heavenly visions and revelations that he was forbid-
den to speak about. "So to keep me from becoming conceited because
of the surpassing greatness of the revelations, a thorn was given me in
the flesh, a messenger of Satan to harass me, to keep me from becoming conceited" (2 Corinthians 12:7). Paul pleaded with the Lord three
times that the thorn be removed, "But he said to me, 'My grace is sufficient for you, for my power is made perfect in weakness'" (12:9).

Most likely, we will not know until heaven whether Satan was
involved in our discipline or trials. It is not necessary for us to know
the exact reason for a trial in order to profit from it. Job *didn't* know that
God and Satan had a conversation about him and that God allowed
Satan to strip him of his family and wealth in order to test his loyalty
to God. However, Paul *did* know that his thorn in the flesh (probably
a chronic painful condition) had come to him from Satan.

Sometimes God allows Satan to ensnare and exploit perpetual
sin that we are not willing to forsake. This can be any sin that has
become an addiction: alcoholism, drugs, pornography, all forms of
sexual immorality, gambling, occult practices, and so on. The devil is
prowling around looking for a weak Christian—one who is not sober-
minded and watchful—whom he may devour (1 Peter 5:8). Because
God knows all things, He may discipline us to lead us to repentance
and prevent us from sinning in an even bigger way in the future.

A pastor once said that we should watch for and welcome God's discipline. [5] And wise King Solomon instructed his son,

> My son, do not despise the LORD's discipline
>   or be weary of his reproof,

> for the LORD reproves him whom he loves,
> as a father the son in whom he delights.
> (Proverbs 3:11-12)

God uses different ways and means of discipline to bring about repentance and restoration. The Holy Spirit convicts us of our sin, and guilt leads us to acknowledge and confess our transgression and claim the cleansing work of Christ (1 John 1:9). It is important to know that after our sin has been confessed and forgiven, guilt is no longer necessary. Any persistence of guilt is the work of Satan and must be rejected in the name of the Lord Jesus Christ.

All sin has consequences of some kind due to God's moral order. "Do not be deceived: God is not mocked, for whatever one sows, that will he also reap" (Galatians 6:7). Based on the laws of sowing and reaping, there are several principles to remember. *First*, some consequences may not appear for a long time and we may think that there are none, but that is due to the fact that we reap in a different season than we sow in. *Second*, we may reap a smaller (less severe) crop than the amount of seed (sin) sown. *Third*, there may be a crop failure. By God's amazing grace and mercy, the consequences may not be noticeable in this life. However, at the judgment seat of Christ, we will receive what we are due for what we have done in this life, whether good or evil (2 Corinthians 5:10).

God hates sin and we must not be foolhardy and take His patience for granted, thinking we can sin and get away with it. We must be careful to not interpret the patience of God as the leniency of God. Through incredible displays of God's mercy, He may lessen the penalty when we confess and forsake our sins. Because of God's amazing grace, we can trust Him to keep His promise in Romans 8:28, "And we know that *for those who love God all things work together for good*, for those who are called according to his purpose."

One consequence that often stays with us long after we have confessed and forsaken our sin is emotional and spiritual trauma. It is possible to experience a despair of the soul resulting from our shame, regret, sorrow, and ongoing consequences. This in itself may be a means of discipline. What can we do when we are overwhelmed by our sorrow? Read the Psalms. There are no more plaintive, mournful words ever written than those of David during two of the most difficult times in his life: throughout the years he was fleeing for his life from King Saul and his enemies, and after he had committed the sins of adultery and murder.

Over and over again David pleads with God to hear his prayers, to be merciful, forgive, comfort, protect, and not forsake or forget him. Psalms 3, 16, 25, 32, 42, and 51 are ones of great loneliness, fear, confession, hope, pleading, and trusting God to forgive and be merciful to him. May you also be comforted and restored as you read the Psalms.

Finally, we must watch for and welcome God's discipline with humility and acceptance. [6] Let us ask God to search our hearts to reveal any sins or failures that might be causing the hardship (Psalm 119:67). May we be willing to learn from every trial whether we know the reason for it or not:

> I know, O Lord, that your rules are righteous,
>   and that in faithfulness you have afflicted me.
>   (Psalm 119:75)

Taking God's Word to Heart

1. What does the discipline of the Lord mean in your life?

2. What is the purpose of discipline and what does it accomplish?

3. In what ways does God discipline His children?

4. Are you aware of God's discipline in your life? If so, in what ways?

DISCIPLINING OUR CHILDREN

Proverbs 13:24 (NIV)—
Whoever spares the rod hates their children,
but the one who loves their children
is careful to discipline them.

Proverbs 29:17 (NIV)—
Discipline your children, and they will give you peace;
they will bring you the delights you desire.

Ephesians 6:4—*Fathers [and mothers], do not*
provoke your children to anger, but bring them up
in the discipline and instruction of the Lord.

The Bible teaches us that we have a great responsibility to discipline our children. From early childhood we must teach them the Holy Scriptures. As Paul reminded Timothy, "from childhood you have been acquainted with the sacred writings, which are able to make you wise for salvation through faith in Christ Jesus" (2 Timothy 3:15). If we withhold discipline, we do not love our children. They will bring shame to us because foolishness is bound up in a child's heart. A disciplined child will become a wise child and will bring delight to us. We discipline them *because* we love them.

We are admonished as parents to correct and teach our children obedience: "Children, obey your parents in the Lord, for this is right" (Ephesians 6:1). Are there any guidelines that can help us to discipline our children well and wisely? In the remainder of this reading, I want to pass along some fundamental characteristics about children, and some of the discipline principles I have found to be the most effective.

The purpose of discipline is to help a child understand and accept a set of values that will shape their character, rather than merely controlling their behavior. The goal of Christian discipline is to instill the qualities of "love, joy, peace, patience, kindness, goodness, faithfulness, gentleness and self-control" (Galatians 5:22-23). Simply put, discipline is helping a child learn healthy self-control. Discipline helps a child learn to do what is right because they understand that it *is* right, not because they are forced or pressured to conform. If we don't teach our children to obey us, they will find it difficult to obey God.

Is there a difference between discipline and punishment? Discipline seeks to instruct and nurture the child into positive action. Punishment seeks revenge or getting even for unacceptable behavior. The parent who merely punishes may show hostility and frustration, which will cause a child to be fearful and feel guilty.

In our tolerant, permissive society *discipline* is a negative word and no longer politically correct. Spanking is considered abusive. The book of Proverbs is regarded as outdated, even though we see evidence of its truth all around us. However, we should not be afraid to discipline our children as God has commanded. A child's sense of justice is violated if he is not disciplined when he knows as well as you do that he has disobeyed and needs correction. Discipline gives children self-respect.

> Whoever spares the rod hates their children,
>> but the one who loves their children is careful to
>> discipline them.
>
>> (Proverbs 13:24 niv)

This is not child abuse—which is wrong and evil—and whoever is guilty of it will answer to God. Abuse demoralizes and crushes the spirit. Discipline that is done in love and patience leads to repentance, joy, and obedience. The goal should not be to merely change our children's behavior, but to change their heart.

Disciplining with "the rod" means to inflict a measure of pain on a disobedient child who understands that he has been disobedient. It is to be done by a parent who is in control of themselves and never in anger. It is wise to reserve spanking for deliberate, defiant disobedience. It should make a child cry, not in anger, but in repentance and submission. We should not spank with our hand because our hands are for showing love, tenderness, and care to our child. Nor should we spank with any object that would cause injury. A ruler or a similar object is appropriate. After making sure that your child understands why they are being spanked, you can administer three to five swats to their behind or their hand.

After the discipline, lead your child in a simple prayer of repentance, "Dear Jesus, I'm sorry for disobeying by (name the offense). Please help me to obey Mommy. Amen." Repentance should be met with words of forgiveness, physical affection, comfort, and the assurance that you love the child.

We have to remember that children will be children—foolish, silly, careless, forgetful, curious, selfish, mean, late, sloppy, easily distracted, and accident prone (lots of them!). Children will spill and drop just about anything liquid—it's part of being a child and learning coordination. If, however, you have instructed the child *not* to touch a container of some liquid, and they pick it up (and spill it), then they have deliberately disobeyed you, and that is worthy of a spanking.

On the other hand, when a child gets distracted by something and forgets to put his crayons and papers back in the drawer when he's finished—as you instructed him to—his behavior does not qualify for a spanking. That was not defiant disobedience. It may be necessary to have your child repeat your instructions back to you so that he understands what you are requiring of him. When a child is old enough to read, you can print out the rules and instructions and display them as a reminder.

Let the discipline fit the offense. There are many ways to apply discipline: time outs, taking away a favorite toy or game (especially if they have failed to put their toys away), removing a privilege such as time playing a computer game or watching their favorite TV program, or missing an activity ("If you finish cleaning your room by 4:30, you may go out to shoot baskets with Jack.").

When you call your children to come to you, teach them to reply, "Coming!" This helps establish respect between you and your child and helps them to remain on task and not get distracted as they obey. In order to get their attention when they are engrossed in something, you can teach them to say, "Yes, Mother [or Father]." If possible, then give your child a moment to change their focus from what they're doing to you.

Verbal authority must be established in order to carry out discipline. Start at the earliest age possible, when they begin to crawl. Elisabeth Elliot gives four simple principles in her video, *A Peaceful Home*:

1. Speak the child's name.

2. Establish eye contact.

3. Speak in a normal tone of voice.

4. Speak only once.

By repeating this pattern over and over, you establish verbal authority. You are telling the child that you are going to speak once and you expect them to obey you quickly, cheerfully, and without grumbling. If you count to three or to ten, you are teaching them that they don't have to obey immediately—only when you reach three or ten. Elisabeth's counsel may sound too strict, but she contends that "delayed obedience is disobedience." A child will test your authority many times, so be consistent each time.

Children need to know what is expected of them. It is helpful for us and protective for the child if we childproof our home by the time they reach the crawling stage. This will focus on positive rather than negative behavior as they explore their world.

Choose age-appropriate rules for your home. Discuss them with each child and make sure they understand the rules and why they are important. When the rules are not consistently applied, children will become confused. It follows then that we make sure children understand what will happen if they break a rule. Again, it is confusing for the child if they break the rule one time and are disciplined, but the next time they break it, there is no discipline. Be consistent.

If we speak in a loud, angry voice, we have lost our self-control and will produce anger and resentment in our child. If frustration, discouragement, or resentment appear in the child that has been disciplined, the method used was inappropriate for that child, no matter how well-intentioned. Some children have gentle spirits that can be easily crushed. Other children are strong-willed and need much firmer, stricter discipline.

Sometimes children will obey but will have a bad attitude, such as disrespect, indifference, carelessness, and anger. A wrong attitude will bring forth unkind words and defiant behavior. It is a matter of the heart. We must take the time to talk it out with our child and find out what they are thinking. Our child may think we have been unfair to them or that we are more lenient with their sibling. They may feel disrespected and unloved. We must be willing to apologize and make anything right that has offended them.

God has given us authority over our children, and they need to know that. Society wants to take away a parent's authority and give it to the schools, teachers, delinquency officers, the courts, and Planned Parenthood. Jesus says, "If anyone causes one of these little ones— those who believe in me—to stumble, it would be better for them to have a large millstone hung around their neck and to be drowned in the depths of the sea" (Matthew 18:6 NIV).

Strong words, indeed, to emphasize the seriousness of leading a child, teenager, or young person into sinful behavior or to abuse them in any way. We and others in authority have a great responsibility to protect, teach, guide, and discipline the children in our care to keep them from sin and turn their hearts toward God.

As children get older, allowing them to experience the natural consequences of their choices is crucial, though often hard. Ruth Graham was once asked what she would do different if she could redo any of her parenting. She said, "I would have 'fixed it' for them less, and allowed them to experience consequences more."

I strongly agree. I didn't want my children to suffer too much, but suffering the consequences of their mistakes taught them lessons they could learn in no other way. Therefore, in many cases, the consequences become the discipline. Teenagers must be disciplined differently than when they were younger. Removing privileges such as driving the car, spending time with friends, using electronics and technology, and attending sports events are more appropriate. Again, it's important to get to the issue of what's going on in their hearts. We need to understand what makes them behave or misbehave as they do. The better we know our child's personality, temperament, fears, gender-based likes and dislikes, the easier it will be to discipline them.

All of our discipline must be covered by much prayer, sometimes agonizing prayer—prayer that fights Satan for the soul of your beloved child. (I recommend an excellent book by Iris Delgado titled *Satan, You Can't Have My Children*.)

A child's body may obey us, but their hearts may be angry and rebellious. Remember that rules without a relationship equal rebellion. Have you established a loving, forgiving, understanding relationship with your child? Have you led them to the cross and explained the gospel, that Jesus loved them enough to die for their sins so they might be forgiven and cleansed and become a new creation in Christ? Obedience brings blessing, and God has promised to enrich the life of an obedient child (Ephesians 6:1-3).

Never give up on a child because God will never give up on you, His child.

Taking God's Word to Heart

1. Why do we discipline our children and for what purpose?

2. Which behaviors call for physical discipline and which do not?

3. Why is verbal authority important? In what ways can we help our children learn to obey?

4. What is the importance of establishing a loving relationship with our children?

ENDURANCE

Hebrews 12:1-4—*Therefore, since we are surrounded by so great a cloud of witnesses, let us also lay aside every weight, and sin which clings so closely, and let us run with endurance the race that is set before us, looking to Jesus, the founder and perfecter of our faith, who for the joy that was set before him endured the cross, despising the shame, and is seated at the right hand of the throne of God. Consider him who endured from sinners such hostility against himself, so that you may not grow weary or fainthearted.*

James 1:12 (NIV)—*Blessed is the one who perseveres under trial because, having stood the test, that person will receive the crown of life that the Lord has promised to those who love him.*

2 Timothy 4:7-8—*I have fought the good fight, I have finished the race, I have kept the faith. Henceforth there is laid up for me the crown of righteousness, which the Lord, the righteous judge, will award to me on that Day, and not only to me but also to all who have loved his appearing.*

Eric Liddell is well-known as the Scottish athlete who won both a gold and a bronze medal in the 1924 Summer Olympics in Paris, as depicted in the Oscar-winning 1981 movie *Chariots of Fire*. Lesser known is his dedicated work as a missionary in China from 1925 to 1943. When Japanese aggression forced British nationals to leave, Eric's wife and children returned to Canada. Later he was interned by the

Japanese at a camp and held there as a prisoner until his death, just five months before liberation.

Throughout all of Eric's hardships and suffering he remained faithful to God in caring for the elderly, teaching Bible classes, playing games with the children, and teaching them science. Though he was often weary and malnourished, he never lost his humor, love for life, and giving himself to minister to others with enthusiasm. Eric Liddell is a picture of one who endured faithfully despite extreme adversity and the deep sorrow over never seeing his family again.

The lesson we learn about endurance from this man is that even in the harshest of circumstances, we can be faithful, joyful, and productive.

Endurance is the ability to withstand hardship or adversity, especially the ability to sustain a prolonged stressful effort or activity, such as a marathon runner's endurance. It is persistence to the end of a trial, hardship, or period of suffering. Sometimes it is surviving against all odds.

The book of James teaches us about endurance: "Dear brothers and sisters, when troubles come your way, consider it an opportunity for great joy. For you know that when your faith is tested, your endurance has a chance to grow. So let it grow, for when your endurance is fully developed, you will be perfect and complete, needing nothing" (James 1:2-4 NLT). Trials test our faith. Tested faith develops endurance within us. Endurance matures us into a Christ-like person—tried and true. God knows that endurance will produce a result that nothing else can. That is why He allows trials and tragedies in our lives.

Trials are inevitable. I have never met anyone who has not gone through at least one difficult experience or tragedy. Years ago a dear woman shared her long and sorrowful story with me. In tears and exhaustion, she concluded, "My whole life is a trial."

Trials come in different varieties: sickness, financial reversals, death of a loved one, broken marriages, cancer, abuse, death of a beloved pet, rebellious children, car accidents, betrayal, false accusations, hurricanes, tornados, fires, floods. The list is endless.

Hebrews 11 has been called "God's Gallery of Heroes" because it lists those, some named and some not, who endured to the end even though many died without seeing the answers to their prayers.

> Some were tortured, refusing to accept release, so that they might rise again to a better life. Others suffered mocking and flogging, and even chains and imprisonment. They were stoned, they were sawn in two, they were killed with the sword. They went about in skins of sheep and goats, destitute, afflicted, mistreated—of whom the world was not worthy—wandering about in deserts and mountains, and in dens and caves of the earth (Hebrews 11:35-38).

We can hardly imagine the horror and cruelty these people suffered. What gave them the ability to endure in the face of such extreme harshness and brutality? Faith. "Now faith is the assurance of things hoped for, the conviction of things not seen. For by it the people of old received their commendation" (Hebrews 11:1-2). They endured suffering unto death because they believed in the promises of God. They died in faith because they believed that God existed, created the universe, and that He would reward those who trusted Him.

How can we develop faith like that? By understanding and accepting these truths about faith: Sometimes it changes our circumstances and sometimes it does not; it does not judge God by our circumstances; it enables us to accept what God gives us rather than what we want; it always leads to ultimate victory. We do not have to win in this life in order to win in the next. Hebrews 11 was not written to teach us how to perform miracles, but how to endure even when we don't see any of them. Faith gives us the endurance to go on believing whether we see a miracle or not. [7]

Moses is an excellent example of one with a long-range view from this life into the next. "By faith Moses, when he was grown up, refused to be called the son of Pharaoh's daughter, choosing rather to be mistreated with the people of God than to enjoy the fleeting pleasures of sin. He considered the reproach of Christ greater wealth than the treasures of Egypt, for he was looking to the reward" (Hebrews 11:24-26). As the leader of the great nation of Israel, Moses endured his complex responsibilities and difficulties by looking to his reward.

The next chapter of Hebrews gives us specific instructions on how to successfully run our race of life: "Therefore, since we are surrounded by so great a cloud of witnesses, let us also lay aside every weight, and sin which clings so closely, and let us run with endurance the race that is set before us" (Hebrews 12:1).

Some people think this "cloud of witnesses" refers to those who have gone to heaven and are now watching us here on earth. But in context, it is clear that the witnesses are the heroes of Hebrews 11, and we are motivated, not because they see us, but because we see them in Scripture. Their faithfulness and obedience should motivate and teach us how to endure our injustices and sufferings. We are to glance at these heroes and then gaze on Jesus.

What are the rules of the race? *First*, we must eliminate all sinful distractions by "laying aside every weight." Some people need to join a spiritual Weight Watchers group. Many things weigh us down—all sin, bad habits, attitudes, and actions that sap our focus, time, and energy from running the race.

Second, we must keep our feet free from the "sin which clings so closely." Sin not only entangles our feet, it comes in the form of debris and potholes along the race track, causing us to stumble. Eventually, it will make us lose the race. Just think of the many people who began with a small weight or sin and ended up wounded on the sideline.

We should especially beware of these sins: bitterness, immorality, idolatry, and ingratitude, which are described in the second half of Hebrews 12. These same sins tempt and overwhelm us today, and we are in danger of being disqualified from the race. Our only hope of winning is to repent. We must ask the Holy Spirit to show us the sins that will keep us from finishing well.

Our best example, however, is Christ Himself: "looking to Jesus, the founder and perfecter of our faith, who for the joy that was set before him endured the cross, despising the shame, and is seated at the right hand of the throne of God" (Hebrews 12:2). Jesus saw beyond the rejection, misunderstanding, false accusations, suffering, shame, and cruel death in His earthly life, and looked instead to the joy and glory that awaited Him in the next.

Hebrews 12 ends with these instructive and encouraging words: "Therefore let us be grateful for receiving a kingdom that cannot be shaken, and thus let us offer to God acceptable worship, with reverence and awe, for our God is a consuming fire" (12:28-29).

Beloved sister, now we know how to endure the trials, temptations, pain, and injustices of our lives:

- by considering the value of trials in forming our character
- by believing the promises of God
- by looking to the joy, reward, and crown that awaits us
- by learning from those in the past who have endured
- by laying aside the weight of all sin that entangles and hinders us
- by fixing our eyes on Jesus
- by not allowing shame to destroy us
- by being grateful for a solid and sure kingdom
- by worshipping God with reverence and awe

A few years ago my dear friend Margaret Nyman began a daily blog *Getting Through This* (which continues to this day) that tracked the challenges and trials she and her husband had gone through as they raised seven children. Over and over again, God sustained and provided for them in amazing ways. Shortly after making a preretirement move to another state, her husband was diagnosed with terminal cancer. She bravely blogged the events of his dramatic decline and excruciating suffering.

The agonizing questions she asked God—the sorrow of the enormous loss her husband's death brought to her and the family—held the rapt attention of thousands of people. Her heart-wrenching honesty showed family, friends, and strangers how she was able to endure this great trial of her faith. There was no miracle, but she endured by keeping her eyes on the goal of the reward and believing that "it would be worth it all" when she would someday see Jesus.

Taking God's Word to Heart

1. How was Jesus able to endure the suffering of the cross and bear the sins of the world?

2. What does the suffering of the saints in Hebrews 11 teach us about enduring hardship?

3. Confess any sin that is weighing you down in your spiritual race and prepare an action plan that will protect you and keep you from that sin.

THE FEAR OF THE LORD

Deuteronomy 5:29— *"Oh that they had such a heart as this always, to fear me and to keep all my commandments, that it might go well with them and with their descendants forever!"*

Psalm 111:10—
The fear of the LORD is the beginning of wisdom; all those who practice it have a good understanding.

Proverbs 1:7—
The fear of the LORD is the beginning of knowledge; fools despise wisdom and instruction.

I spoke to a woman who chose to leave her husband and children to chase her dream. I warned her that she would not only face the consequences, but that since she was a Christian, she would also be displeasing God, and He would discipline her. To my surprise, she answered casually, "Sometimes you have to do what you have to do and deal with God and the devil tomorrow." Although she was a believer, she was acting as those who have "no fear of God before their eyes" (Romans 3:18).

We don't hear much about the fear of the Lord today because we have created in our minds the image of a God who cares for us, understands our weaknesses, and will overlook our sins. Many Christians are convinced there is nothing about God that we should fear. Besides, we live under grace where our sins, past and present, are covered by the blood of Christ, and so we reason that it is safe to sin. What is there to fear? As one person confessed, "Yes, of course, I'm living in sin, but God will forgive me. That is His job."

There is a widespread misconception that the fear of the Lord is an Old Testament concept—that the people had to fear God because they were immediately punished for their sins. But now that Christ has paid for our sin, there is no longer any need to fear God. We should have reverence for God, but we shouldn't actually *fear* Him. In fact, some have accepted the notion that the God of the Old Testament was a wrathful God, but the God of the New is gracious, forgiving, and tolerant. They think that God is more tolerant of sin now than He was in the Old Testament.

In our culture there is a great tolerance of sin and a redefinition of sin. What God says is wrong is being called right, and what God says is right is being called wrong. When we fear God, we hate what He hates—sin. Many believers don't really fear God because they don't know Him very well. They live a casual kind of Christianity, thinking that God is tolerant and their mistakes aren't really sin. After all, Jesus has their back because He died on the cross to forgive them.

There are forty-three references in the New Testament to the fear of God, which is as many as there are to the love of God. So what is taught about God in the New Testament is completely consistent with the Old Testament since God is unchangeable (Malachi 3:6). In fact, we are warned that if we take advantage of God's grace and trivialize our sin, we will have greater judgment under the New Covenant than under the Old (Hebrews 12:25-29). Since we have greater light in the New Testament, we have greater responsibility. Hebrews 12 ends with the ominous words, "for our God is a consuming fire."

With characteristic clarity, Dietrich Bonhoeffer wrote:

> We have become so accustomed to the idea of divine love
> and of God's coming at Christmas that we no longer feel
> the shiver of fear that God's coming should arouse in us.

We are indifferent to the message, taking only the pleasant and agreeable out of it and forgetting the serious aspect that the God of this world draws near to the people of our little earth and lays claim to us. [8]

Jesus gave us this warning, "I tell you, my friends, do not fear those who kill the body, and after that have nothing more that they can do. But I will warn you whom to fear: fear him who, after he has killed, has authority to cast into hell. Yes, I tell you, fear him!" (Luke 12:4-5). If we fear anything other than God, we are deceived. God is the only being in the universe worthy of fear, as stated in Isaiah 8:13 (NIV),

> The LORD Almighty is the one you are to regard as holy,
>> he is the one you are to fear,
>> he is the one you are to dread.

Satan wants us to fear him more than we fear God, but those "in Christ" have been purchased out from under Satan's tyranny and need not fear him any longer.

Most unbelievers do not fear God. They don't know Him; they regard Him as unimportant. They don't realize that He is holy and that the commandments they are constantly breaking are a reflection of who He is. They may feel guilty because of their behavior and some of the consequences, but they don't want God messing with their lives and telling them what to do.

What is the fear of the Lord? The Hebrew meaning is reverent fear, terror, or dread, as we saw in Isaiah 8:13. The fear of the Lord is a reverential awe of God—a reverence for His holiness, power, and glory. It is also a proper respect for His anger toward sin (Isaiah 57:16-17). The fear of the Lord involves knowing who God is, His attributes. It is respect for the power of God's Word. We should stand in awe that God spoke and it was done.

The fear of the Lord brings with it many blessings: It is the key to knowledge and wisdom (Proverbs 1:7). It is the beginning of wisdom and leads to understanding (Psalm 111:10). It leads to life, rest, and satisfaction (Proverbs 19:23). It gives us confidence and provides security and refuge; it is a fountain of life (Proverbs 14:26-27).

What are the practical benefits of fearing the Lord? *First*, we will understand the fear of the Lord and find the knowledge of God, if we seek for wisdom like searching for hidden treasure (Proverbs 2:1-5). Oh, how we desperately need wisdom! Those who fear God are going to be smarter and wiser, especially in applying knowledge and wisdom. A wise woman will fear God and seek His counsel; she will not be hasty in making decisions regarding whom she should marry, her career, how she raises her children, or her choice of friends.

Second, we will have a deeper appreciation of the salvation Jesus came to bring us. We have been saved from the coming wrath of God (1 Thessalonians 1:10). When we have a better understanding of God's anger toward sin, we have a much deeper appreciation for the fact that Jesus died in our place so that we could be acquitted of our sins. Thus, the fear of the Lord enhances our worship, adoration, and thanksgiving to God. The fear of the Lord helps us appreciate that if we were to stand before God on the basis of our own record, we would be condemned. No wonder we are asked to "stand in awe of Him" (Psalm 22:23).

Third, we will have a healthy fear of disobeying God. To fear God means that we recognize that God hates sin and will discipline His sons and daughters if they regard sin lightly by taking advantage of His grace and mercy. God disciplines those He loves; He does not shield His children from the consequences of their careless attitude toward sin. Where the fear of the Lord rules in the heart, there will be a constant conscientious care to keep His commandments: not just to talk about them, but to do them. The fear of the Lord should drive us toward Him, not away from Him.

The fear of the Lord does not come naturally, it must be learned through knowing Him and His attributes. That's why we study theology: "theo" is God and "logy" is logos (or word), and when put together they mean "a word about God." The goal is to seek God by becoming a student of God. We do this by developing an intimate relationship with Him through Bible study, memorizing and meditating on the Word, worshipping and praising Him, and talking to God in prayer every day. As our understanding of Him increases, so will our obedience, devotion, and reverential fear.

Fearing the Lord does not contradict the command to love Him, for our fear is not that of a slave to a harsh master but like that of a child to a Father who is loved and respected. A true fear and reverence for God will prevent us from taking His love and forgiveness for granted and from ignoring His Word by filling our spare time with pleasure and entertainment.

A proper, mature fear of God is having a healthy reverence and respect for the most powerful Being in the universe and the laws He has put in place for our protection and benefit. We fear God and keep His commandments *because* He is love.

May pursuing knowledge of the Holy One become our priority and passion. Every day, may we remember the words of God through Moses to His people Israel, "Oh that they had such a heart as this always, to fear me and to keep all my commandments, that it might go well with them and with their descendants forever!" (Deuteronomy 5:29).

Taking God's Word to Heart

1. What does it mean to fear the Lord?

2. What is the difference between how God dealt with sin in the Old Testament and in the New Testament? Is God more tolerant of sin today?

3. How do we develop a proper fear of the Lord?

4. What difference will having a proper fear of the Lord make in our lives?

FORGIVENESS

Matthew 6:12,14-15—*"Give us this day our daily bread,*
and forgive us our debts,
as we also have forgiven our debtors...

For if you forgive others their trespasses, your heavenly Father
will also forgive you, but if you do not forgive others their
trespasses, neither will your Father forgive your trespasses."

Ephesians 4:32—*Be kind to one another, tenderhearted,*
forgiving one another, as God in Christ forgave you.

Forgiveness is defined as releasing someone from the guilt or penalty of an offense, canceling their debt, and relinquishing our resentment. We can decide to walk away from the offense and behave as though it never happened. We choose to not make the guilty pay for their offense. It is absorbing the hurt and letting the other person go free.

To not forgive is to sin. A licensed marriage and family counselor said, "One reason many Christians don't forgive is they don't grasp the seriousness of it in God's eyes." [9]

We find this truth embedded in the parable Jesus told in Matthew 18:23-35. A king was going to throw one of his servants into prison because he owed him an enormous amount of money, which he could not pay back. The servant begged the king to be patient with him and he would pay the amount, but the king knew it was impossible for him to do so. Out of pity, the king released the servant from the debt and let him go free.

On the way home, the servant met a fellow servant who owed him a small amount of money. He grabbed the man and said, "Pay what you owe." The servant fell down and pleaded with him for patience until he could pay, but the forgiven servant threw his friend in prison until he could pay the debt.

When fellow servants saw what happened, they were distressed and reported to the king what had taken place. The king sent for the servant and said, "You wicked servant! I forgave you all that debt because you pleaded with me. And should not you have had mercy on your fellow servant, as I had mercy on you?" (18:32-33). The angry king delivered the guilty servant to the jailers until he could pay all his debt.

What happens within us when we are unwilling to forgive someone their trespasses or debts against us? It's like a cancer eating away at our souls, destroying relationships and even cutting off the flow of God's grace to us. Robertson McQuilkin comments, "If I insist on dredging up the bitter sludge of some past offense, it is my own spirit that becomes poisoned. The world is filled with wounded Christians who refuse to let the guilty person go, only to find that they are the ones who are bound, shut off from loving relationships, forever turbulent within." [10]

When we say, "I can't forgive," we're really saying, "I won't forgive." Unforgiveness will make us spiritually, psychologically, and sometimes physically sick. Studies show that hanging on to anger and resentment increases our chances of a heart attack, cancer, high blood pressure, and many chronic illnesses. To carry a grudge is like being stung to death by one bee. [11] It doesn't make sense that a forgiven person would withhold forgiveness from someone else.

Why is forgiveness so important to God? It's because we have been graced with the free gift of undeserved forgiveness. We have been given so much grace that we must not refuse to grace others. Forgiving is a natural part of God's character—who He is—and He tells us to be like Him and to forgive. It's impossible to forget what lies behind if you don't let God's grace cover it. He remembers our sin no more, as far as the east is from the west. When you grasp that truth and gain an appreciation of what Jesus's blood does, it will help you to forgive as God forgives us—meaning no hurt is too strong to release to God's grace. [12]

Forgiveness is the reason that God came into the world as a human to reconcile us to Himself. Jesus forgave—forgave when He alone was the only One who had a right to condemn. And if He is willing to forgive us when our sins caused His death, can we, who have so grievously sinned against Him, withhold forgiveness from others? [13]

Jesus was guilty of nothing as He hung on the cross dying for our sins—nothing except being the Son of God and being equal to God. His murderers were guilty of carrying out an evil plot to get rid of Him. But Jesus compassionately said, "Father, forgive them, for they know not what they do" (Luke 23:34). He asked His Father to forgive those who had abused Him and put Him on a cross to die because He knew they did not realize that through their evil, they were accomplishing God's plan of salvation for the human race.

Let us consider a painful possibility: that the evil deeds done against you and me were done by those who didn't realize how horrible their actions were, how it would affect our lives, and that perhaps they were carrying out God's plan of suffering for us. What do we do with the evil and hurt God allows?

Joseph in the Old Testament was cruelly sold by his brothers to a caravan of Ishmaelites on their way to Egypt. Many years later, after he had revealed himself to them, he said, "And now do not be distressed or angry with yourselves because you sold me here, for God sent me before you to preserve life…So it was not you who sent me here, but God" (Genesis 45:5,8).

Some events may be too painful to forget, but we can still forgive and give up our resentment and hatred. In the midst of painful circumstances and incomprehensible events, let us not forget that God is good and that in the end He can make all things work together for our good and for His glory. [14]

True forgiveness of others will create a love that replaces hatred. [15]

God displayed the greatest love of all when He sent His precious Son to be a sacrifice for our sins. It is an astounding truth that only a holy, all-powerful God could orchestrate—at great personal cost—to erase all the filth from our lives and treat us as clean. It is equally amazing, that He tells us to follow His example: "Be kind to one another, tenderhearted, forgiving one another, as God in Christ forgave you" (Ephesians 4:32; Colossians 3:13). Jesus repeatedly warns that if we do not forgive, He will not forgive us. [16]

Forgiving someone who's done you wrong is not condoning what they did nor absolving them of guilt. It is not forgetting but letting go of anger and hurt and moving on. It also decreases the desire for revenge and wanting to make someone suffer for what they did. Psychologically, it eliminates feelings of anxiety and depression and boosts self-esteem. [17]

Do you feel that the sin done against you, or the sin that you yourself committed, is unforgiveable? Adultery, abuse, addiction, abortion. Does it seem as though you're walking around with a scarlet letter *A* on your front? Is the shame and sorrow of your past or present eating away at your soul?

We cannot take justice into our own hands; that belongs to God. It has been said that unforgiveness is like drinking poison but expecting the other person to die. It slowly destroys you, not the person who hurt you. If Jesus can forgive others, so can you. If Jesus can forgive you, then it is arrogant to think that you cannot forgive yourself.

The words of this old hymn give us the right answer:

> What can wash away my sin?
> Nothing but the blood of Jesus.
> What can make me whole again?
> Nothing but the blood of Jesus.

That is why Jesus died—to wash away our sin. Jesus died long before we sinned. Our sin is precisely *why* He died, so that it could be washed away and forgiven.

Why do we struggle so much with forgiving others? For some

people, to forgive is like going to the bank and canceling their account. They would have nowhere to go to win an argument. They would have nothing to draw on—nothing to sustain their anger and hurt. To forgive is to ask them to pick up a building and carry it across the street. They can't or won't do it.

Forgiveness is not easy. It can be an excruciating exercise of the soul—like having a tooth pulled without an anesthetic. We may have to force ourselves to forgive even if we don't feel like it. *But right feelings will follow right actions.* Even though it involves our emotions, it is an act of our will—it is a choice.

To our human way of thinking, it doesn't seem fair and right, but it is so very important. Forgiveness is imperative for our well-being, and we will never be free until we do it. It is a process that we have to repeat over and over throughout our lives.[18] Peter asked Jesus, "'Lord, how often will my brother sin against me, and I forgive him? As many as seven times?' Jesus said to him, 'I do not say to you seven times, but seventy-seven times'" (Matthew 18:21-22).

Long ago I realized that whatever sin I didn't confess or forgive—and there was much from my childhood to forgive—I would pass on to my children. This really scared me. I realized some sinful attitudes had been passed on to me from my parents, and I did not want to see my children suffer and struggle with the same sins. How awful that would be for this to continue into future generations. Reconciliation is not always possible, but forgiveness is.

As a prisoner and survivor of a Nazi concentration camp, Corrie ten Boom had a lot to forgive her captors and tormentors for, including the death of her beloved sister, Betsy. Yet she spoke these words, "To forgive is to set a prisoner free and to discover the prisoner was you."

Taking God's Word to Heart

1. Why is forgiveness so important to God? Why is it so difficult to forgive?

2. What happens within us when we are unwilling to forgive someone who has wronged us?

3. What does Joseph's response to his brothers in Genesis 50:15-21 mean to you? How does the truth of his words help you?

4. Someone will pay the price for your sins. Will it be you or Jesus? Have you accepted Christ's sacrifice on the cross to forgive your sins?

GIVING THANKS

Psalm 50:23—*The one who offers
thanksgiving as his sacrifice glorifies me.*

Psalm 118:1—*Oh give thanks to the* Lord, *for he
is good; for his steadfast love endures forever!*

Colossians 2:6-7—*Therefore, as you received
Christ Jesus the Lord, so walk in him, rooted and
built up in him and established in the faith, just as
you were taught, abounding in thanksgiving.*

1 Thessalonians 5:18—*Give thanks in all circumstances;
for this is the will of God in Christ Jesus for you.*

Giving thanks changes everything, especially us. Giving thanks honors God by reaffirming His sovereignty. When we give thanks for all things, both good and bad, we affirm that He is in charge of all that takes place in His universe. No, we do not give thanks for evil, but we give thanks for how God will make all things work together for good for those who love Him.

Thankful people are generous because they recognize that all they have was not the result of their own efforts. God enabled them to obtain what they have by blessing them with good health, an intelligent mind, and a good work ethic. They also recognize that many people helped them along the way. All that we have is a gift from God that we really don't deserve.

Those who have a generous spirit don't hoard blessing; they are willing to share it with others through giving their time, money, and resources. We learn to be generous by developing a divine perspective, believing and trusting that our heavenly Father knows what we need better than we do. It is learned by realizing there is a divine purpose in our needs and learning to trust God to provide them. We don't have to have all the answers to our questions in order to be thankful. We must learn to live well within the seasons of our lives—some with need and want, and some with abundance.

If we begin our prayers immediately asking God to do this and that for us and for others, then we need to take time to be instructed in biblical praying. The apostle Paul tells us, "Do not be anxious about anything, but *in everything by prayer and supplication with thanksgiving* let your requests be made known to God. And the peace of God, which surpasses all understanding, will guard your hearts and your minds in Christ Jesus" (Philippians 4:6-7). God honors praying that begins with thanksgiving as we bring our requests to Him. Then, we have a promise that all the things we're feeling anxious about will be calmed and comforted by the peace of God. When we pray about everything with thanksgiving, our burdens become lighter and our minds become peaceful.

Ungratefulness affects our lives in many ways. *First*, we are sinning by being disobedient to God and His Word. *Second*, it discredits God's character by declaring that He isn't trustworthy or faithful. *Third*, it gives Satan an opportunity to influence our feelings negatively and enter our thoughts with lies that deceive us. Just as he did in the Garden of Eden when he tricked Adam and Eve, the devil twists truth and lies to us about God and His goodness. *Fourth*, it causes us to look at everything with a negative attitude and fosters complaining and bitterness. *Fifth*, it prevents us from being able to constructively look at difficult situations to see how we can change them with what we already know and have.

What does giving thanks do for us and how does it change us? Giving thanks:

- brings peace and contentment
- changes our countenance and outlook
- drives away selfishness, complaining, and the give-me attitude
- keeps us from saying hurtful words of criticism and negativity
- is like putting on a pair of glasses, enabling us to see and appreciate things we can't normally see when we're ungrateful

We can develop an attitude of gratitude by *choosing* to be thankful. We don't have to feel like giving thanks in order to give thanks. Right feelings will follow right actions. Giving thanks changes the atmosphere and influences others, especially our husband and children, to be thankful for all the past and present blessings in our lives.

Living in gratitude and thanksgiving builds faith in our hearts and enables us to trust God to work all things together for good. It prepares us for the big trials and sorrows that God allows to come into our lives, such as cancer, chronic illness, a disabling accident, natural disasters, divorce, and loss of any kind.

Living like this prepared Scott and Janet Willis for unimaginable horror and loss—the sudden death of six of their children as they drove on a Wisconsin expressway. The gas tank of their van exploded immediately after they drove over a piece of metal that had fallen from a flatbed semitrailer truck in front of them. Though they were able to escape as the fire roared up from the back of the van, they were unable to reach and save their children. As they stood badly burned and in shock and disbelief on the side of the road, Scott said to Janet, "'I will bless the LORD at all times; his praise shall continually be in my mouth.' Janet, God has been preparing us for this our whole lives." Theirs is an incredible story of sorrow, pain, suffering, and adjustment, but God has been faithful to carry them through a long, arduous healing process to peace and acceptance. Years later, Janet tenderly said, "Though I miss them terribly, I know my children are always good, happy, and safe in heaven with Jesus."

What spiritual actions can we take to develop an attitude of gratitude?

- Acknowledge that we are ungrateful and discontent and that it is sin.
- Ask God to show us why we're ungrateful and confess all known sin.
- Ask God to change our attitude and give us a heart of thanksgiving.
- Cultivate a consistent daily quiet time of prayer, Bible reading, and study.
- Memorize Scripture that will renew our minds with truth.
- Resist Satan by affirming God's goodness and mighty power in our life.
- Read psalms of praise, and sing and listen to praise music.
- Begin a list of blessings and things to be thankful for and add to it daily.
- Thank God for the endless spiritual blessings we have in Christ, such as grace, salvation, forgiveness, mercy, love, wisdom, peace: "I will give thanks to the LORD with my whole heart; I will recount all of your wonderful deeds" (Psalm 9:1).
- When there is a need, pray with thanksgiving and faith that God will supply it.

Have you ever prayed, "Lord, make me satisfied with what I have right now"? When we choose to deal seriously with our sin of ungratefulness by pursuing God and trusting Him, we will find our desire for the things of this world will dramatically decrease. Paul tells us, "But godliness with contentment is great gain, for we brought nothing into the world and we cannot take anything out of the world. But if we have food and clothing, with these we will be content" (1 Timothy 6:6-8).

Sometimes we may confuse spiritual needs with our emotional, physical, and psychological needs. The following ideas are practical actions we can take to foster an attitude of gratitude.

- Develop a support system of trusted friends to talk to, go out to lunch with, and do some fun activities with.
- Hire a babysitter or use a mom's day out to get away for a couple of hours.
- Watch less TV, which will eliminate commercials and ungodly situations and solutions.
- Get more sleep and eat healthy food.
- Become organized and clean your house.
- Paint a room and rearrange it.
- Join a weight-loss program and stick with it.
- Collaborate with a friend or another mom to start a home business, such as cleaning houses, tutoring kids, or helping disabled and elderly people in their homes with light housework, laundry, taking them grocery shopping, or running errands.
- Choose one minor and one major need in your life that you have the power and resources to change.
- Change what you can, accept what you can't, and give the rest to God.

Even children can teach us how we can be thankful in the midst of sorrow and trials. On her husband's birthday, Lisa Beamer was feeling intense sorrow. Todd had been on the plane that crashed into a field in

Pennsylvania on 9/11 and had shouted, "Let's roll!" as he helped to prevent the terrorists from slamming it into a building in our nation's capital. Their eight-year-old son asked his mother why she felt so sad, to which she replied, "Because your dad isn't here to celebrate his birthday." As only a child could, he asked, "But we can still have cake, can't we?"

Yes, when the bottom falls out of our lives, when we've lost our dearest friend, when there isn't enough money in our bank account to pay the mortgage or rent...we can still give thanks. We can still connect with friends, we can still worship with other believers, we can still help those who are more needy.

And we can still eat cake!

Taking God's Word to Heart

1. Why are we ungrateful and discontent, and what does that reveal about us?

2. What are some results of being ungrateful?

3. Why should we give thanks in everything?

4. What actions can we take to develop a life of thanksgiving?

GOD'S LOVE FOR US

Romans 8:38-39—*For I am sure that neither death nor life, nor angels nor rulers, nor things present nor things to come, nor powers, nor height nor depth, nor anything else in all creation, will be able to separate us from the love of God in Christ Jesus our Lord.*

1 John 4:9-10—*In this the love of God was made manifest among us, that God sent his only Son into the world, so that we might live through him. In this is love, not that we have loved God but that he loved us and sent his Son to be the propitiation for our sins.*

Many women do not believe God loves them. Yes, they know the Scripture that tells us God loves the world and sent His only Son Jesus to die for our sins. But truth be told, He just doesn't love *them* personally and passionately. They feel unlovable for various reasons: too bad...too good...too broken...too angry...too poor...too rich...too fat...too abused...too sick...too rebellious...too rejected.

With joy and hope, the real truth is that Jesus's love for us is the greatest love story of all the ages—not of a man and a woman but of the God-man and *every* woman. Not an ordinary romance, as wonderful as that can be, but a spiritual romance with the One who created us. Jesus knows all about us and yet loves us unconditionally, sacrificially, and passionately.

What great love stories come to your mind? Every little girl knows about Cinderella and the miserable life she had at the hands of her cruel stepmother and mean stepsisters. She was the most unlikely girl to show up at the royal ball, for she had nothing and her only friends were the little creatures of nature. Even though she had some unusual help in getting dressed and being transported there, she had no guarantee she would meet the prince, let alone dance with him. What a delightful ending that the handsome prince searched for and rescued Cinderella, and they lived happily ever after. Many women think this happens only in fairy tales.

Consider the Old Testament story of Ruth, a poor, brokenhearted widow. All she had was a bitter mother-in-law whose husband and sons had died. Ruth loved her dearly and decided to go with Naomi as she returned to her homeland of Bethlehem. As a foreigner in that land, Ruth followed Naomi's wise instruction and went to work for Boaz, a good and honest businessman who was her mother-in-law's distant relative. Ruth kept herself pure and waited for God's plan to unfold. It's quite a love story—full of cultural intrigue—of a grieving woman who made a journey, laid aside her pride to work in the fields, and found hope and an amazing new life. Of all the women available to Boaz, he chose Ruth to be his wife, and she became part of the lineage of Jesus Christ.

And then there's Jane Austen's classic novel *Pride and Prejudice* set in early nineteenth-century England. It's the story of the Bennet family of five daughters from a lower economic and social status. The possibility of all of them finding husbands of means who could provide for them was slim. It has a fascinating plot with many relational twists and turns.

The main character is Elizabeth, the second-born daughter, who is intelligent, witty, and attractive. At a social ball where eligible young men and women are introduced to one another, she meets the quiet, serious Mr. Darcy, who is a rich man but socially withdrawn. Over a period of time in various settings they become friends, and she tries to draw him out. However, he is preoccupied with his social standing and wealth. She is told something false about him, and thinking he is a mean, selfish, proud man, rejects his proposal of love. She eventually discovers the truth about him and the way he has used his wealth to help many people.

In the end, both Mr. Darcy and Elizabeth lay aside their pride and prejudice and acknowledge their love for each other. Though her gown is plain and worn and she has no dowry, she accepts his love, wealth, and offer of marriage.

Beloved women, this is really our story—God pursuing us, poor and sinful, with His love and wealth. Sometimes we have false beliefs about Him and often feel unworthy of His love. We can't imagine that the God who created all things would love us personally and want to have a divine relationship with us. But women were created to be loved, by man and by God. When sin came into the world, everything changed. Sin destroyed the original relationship Adam and Eve enjoyed with each other and with God in the Garden of Eden. (By the way, Eve is the only woman who could truly say, "I have nothing to wear!")

While I was meditating on God's love, it occurred to me that God shows His love for us in much the same way that a husband would, or *should*. Sadly, many husbands are self-absorbed, busy, tired, or occupied with other interests. But that is never true of God. Here are some of the many ways God demonstrates His love for us:

> Listens, appreciates, speaks kindly, tells you He loves you, does special things, satisfies longings, forgives, shows compassion, understands, comforts, blesses, encourages, respects, is always available, is generous, surprises you with gifts, holds your hand, holds you close to His heart, spends time, helps, cares, provides, stays close by, walks with you, defends and protects, writes love notes.

A husband who does only a few of these things is highly desirable. But God wants to do all of them for us, if we will allow Him to. He loves us so much and wants us to believe, trust, and obey Him. "See what kind of love the Father has given to us, that we should be called children of God; and so we are" (1 John 3:1).

God has written us a love letter—the Bible. It is the story of the human race and God's divine intervention. Profound. Deep. Mysterious. Life-giving. It brings hope into our human existence that Jesus stepped out of eternity and heaven and entered our world. He did for us what no mere human could do. He became the God-man and died on a cross, taking the punishment we deserve for our sin and the punishment for all the sin done against us. The Bible tells us so clearly how much God loves us:

> "For God so loved the world, that he gave his only Son, that whoever believes in him should not perish but have eternal life" (John 3:16).

> This is how we know what love is: Jesus Christ laid down his life for us. (1 John 3:16 NIV).

> But God shows his love for us in that while we were still sinners, Christ died for us (Romans 5:8).

In the New Testament there are several accounts of how Jesus showed His love, acceptance, and compassion for women. He chose these women because they were desperate. They had exhausted all human resources, and all of them needed a miraculous intervention. Some of them had great faith; some of them had no faith. But every one of them had a divine encounter with Jesus.

For some, He went a great distance to where they were so *they* could find Him. For others, He allowed them to be brought to Him so *He* could find them. He asked them personal questions He already knew the answers to. He tested their knowledge and faith. He questioned them to reveal their stories and what was in their hearts. The holy Son of God knew all about them and yet did not condemn them.

To the divorced woman, Jesus offered living water—*salvation*—and invited her to worship Him in spirit and in truth (John 4:4-26).

To the desperate mother, Jesus said, "O woman, great is your faith!

Be it done for you as you desire." And her daughter was *healed and delivered* from demon-possession (Matthew 15:21-28).

To the immoral woman who wiped His feet with her hair as she poured perfume and wept tears of repentance, Jesus said, "Your sins are *forgiven*" (Luke 7:36-50).

To the chronically ill woman suffering from bleeding, Jesus said, "Daughter, your faith has made you *well*; go in *peace,* and be *healed* of your disease" (Mark 5:24-34).

To the woman caught in adultery and brought to Him in the temple, Jesus said, "*Neither do I condemn you; go,* and from now on sin no more" (John 8:3-11).

To Mary Magdalene, from whom He had cast out seven demons, bringing her out of a prison of darkness into *light* and *freedom,* Jesus gently called her name, "Mary," as she stood near the garden tomb (John 20:11-18).

To His friend Martha, who was worried and anxious, He showed her what was in her heart, and said, "You are *anxious and troubled about many things,* but one thing is necessary. Mary has chosen the good portion, which will not be taken away from her" (Luke 10:38-42).

Of His friend Mary (Martha's sister), who anointed Jesus prior to His impending death with expensive perfume and wiped His feet with her hair, He said, "*Leave her alone,* so that she may keep it for the day of my burial" (John 12:1-8).

When we take time to study these biblical accounts, it is astonishing to see the love, care, and interest Jesus had for these women. He went out of His way and positioned Himself to be in their way so that He could change their lives. He pursued them. No one was too sinful, too demon-possessed, too sick, too poor, too worried, or had too little faith or too many divorces. He accepted and loved them just as they were.

Beloved reader, do you realize that Jesus loves you just like that?

You see, God's love does not depend on anything we can do or cannot do. He doesn't withdraw His love when we sin. To be sure, He is grieved and waits for us to confess our sin so He can forgive and restore our fellowship. But no sin is greater than His grace and love. He doesn't love us less when we sin. He doesn't love us more when we obey, though life is much better and joyful when we do. God's love depends on His character and His choice to love sinful human beings. The Word of God declares over and over that God demonstrated His love to us through His Son Jesus Christ. It is more than just believing this truth by faith, it is being willing to let go of anything that stands in the way and lies to us that we are unworthy of His love.

Have you had a divine encounter with this same Jesus? He can do for you what no one else can do. What do you desperately need from Him today? His free gift of living water and salvation? Forgiveness? Deliverance? Healing? Cleansing? Restoration? Freedom? Fellowship? Hope? Peace? Encouragement? Love?

It is time to be honest with yourself and with God. Are you willing to answer this hard question: What is the most difficult thing in my life that is holding me back from experiencing the pure, glorious love of Jesus?

Your answer cannot be about anyone else, such as your husband, ex-husband, child, mother, father, boss, friend, the person who abused you, a tragic event, disability, illness, or any circumstance. Your answer must be about *you*: your unbelief, anger, stubbornness, rebellion, lust, immorality, unforgiveness, hatred, bitterness, wrong attitudes, or ungratefulness.

People, events, or circumstances don't make us angry and bitter. Rather, our own sin, reaction, or attitudes hurt us and keep us imprisoned in our world of pain and hopelessness.

Beth Moore has said, "The prison door unlocks from the inside." We can choose to forgive and let go of pain, anger, and bitterness—no matter what caused it—and stop blaming anyone or anything. We can be free to accept and experience Jesus's love.

Do you hear Him gently speaking your name? He is calling you "beloved daughter." Henri Nouwen describes Jesus's voice, "The spiritual life is a life in which you gradually learn to listen to a voice that says, 'You are the beloved and on you my favour rests.' I want to hear that voice. It is not a very loud voice because it is an intimate voice. It comes from a very deep place. It is soft and gentle."

Can you say, "Jesus loves me, this I know"? More than anything I could hope for or give to you, my prayer is for you to know and to find delight in the pure love of Jesus.

Taking God's Word to Heart

1. Why do we think God doesn't love us? How do we *know* that God in Jesus Christ loves us?

2. How can Jesus love us when He knows everything about us? How does He show His love for us?

3. What might God show you that is hindering your acceptance of His love?

4. What actions can you take so you can experience God's love more completely and deeply?

GRACE

Ephesians 1:6-8—*To the praise of his glorious grace, with which he has blessed us in the Beloved. In him we have redemption through his blood, the forgiveness of our trespasses, according to the riches of his grace, which he lavished upon us, in all wisdom and insight.*

Ephesians 2:8-9—*For by grace you have been saved through faith. And this is not your doing; it is the gift of God, not a result of works, so that no one may boast.*

2 Corinthians 12:9—*But he said to me, "My grace is sufficient for you, for my power is made perfect in weakness." Therefore I will boast all the more gladly of my weaknesses, so that the power of Christ may rest upon me.*

What is grace and how do we know when we have it? Is it automatic? How does a believer appropriate and experience God's grace? Is it reserved for certain trials? Is it available for only a few godly people?

Grace is God's kindness and undeserved favor—while we were dead in our sins, Jesus Christ died for us. Adam and Eve died spiritually when they disobeyed God, plunging the human race into a state of sinfulness, for all have sinned and fall short of God's glory (Romans 3:23). We are all dead in our sin—helpless—unable to do anything to save ourselves. Dead people cannot earn their salvation. "But God, being rich in mercy, because of the great love with which he loved us, even when we were dead in our trespasses, made us alive together with

Christ—*by grace* you have been saved" (Ephesians 2:4-5). Through Jesus's death and shed blood on the cross, we are justified—made right with God—by His free gift of grace (Ephesians 2:8-9). We do not deserve nor can we ever earn God's grace. That is why grace is so amazing.

We are redeemed—released from the debt of our sin—by His rich, glorious grace. Salvation is no longer based on works of obedience, as it was in the Old Testament, otherwise, grace would no longer be grace (Romans 11:6). God's grace is available to everyone who believes *through faith* (also supplied by God). When we cry out for His mercy and forgiveness, God's grace restores what the human race lost in the Garden of Eden—spiritual life and fellowship with our Creator.

The New Testament frequently speaks of the "grace of our Lord Jesus Christ." Grace is His signature across our lives that He gave His blood to redeem us. We should rejoice every day for the grace of God that has saved us from His wrath and the penalty our sins deserve. The words of the first verse of the beloved hymn "Amazing Grace" express it so well:

> Amazing grace, how sweet the sound,
> That saved a wretch like me.
> I once was lost, but now am found,
> Was blind, but now I see.

It is normal to wish we had more of God's grace because life is often hard, unpredictable, painful, lonely, unjust, and tragic. The human race is worried by fear of terrorism, economic collapse, and natural disasters.

Oh, how we need grace to live on this earth. I am thankful that God doesn't save us and then leave us to struggle through life on our own. After salvation, grace and mercy keep on working for us. God tells us clearly in Hebrews 4:16 how to claim more grace for our trials and suffering: "Let us then with confidence draw near to the throne of grace, that we may receive mercy and find grace to help in time of need."

This is a profound and sure promise from our heavenly Father that He will give us grace whenever we need it. But it is not a frivolous promise. Every word is significant and instructive. *Let*—ability and authority. *Us*—every believer. *With confidence*—certainty that He will do what He said; a holy boldness. *Draw near*—specific action by means of sincere prayer. *To the throne of grace*—take time to bow and linger in this holy place. *That we may receive*—personal assurance that it will happen. *Mercy*—compassion, relief. *And find grace*—discover a treasure of God's kindness, help, reprieve, blessing, and love. *To help*—assist, support, relieve. *In time of need*—any generation, season, moment, or circumstance of necessity, pain, suffering, fear, or hardship.

Could it be any clearer? How often have we carelessly asked God for grace and mercy and then wondered why we didn't receive any? The key is that through prayer we seek for what we need God's way, not our way.

The apostle Paul tells us in 2 Corinthians 12 that fourteen years earlier he had received visions and great revelations from God. "So to keep me from becoming conceited because of the surpassing greatness of the revelations, a thorn was given me in the flesh, a messenger of Satan to harass me" (12:7). Commentators have suggested that this thorn was possibly poor eyesight, malaria fever, severe migraine headaches, or demonic harassment. Whatever it was, it must have been painful. Paul prayed three times that it be taken from him, and when God finally spoke, the message was, "My grace is sufficient for you, for my power is made perfect in weakness" (12:9).

There are two ways to carry a heavy load: one is to make the load lighter; the other is to be given the strength to bear it. God told Paul that in this instance the thorn would not leave him, but that grace would be given so he could bear it. As a result, this thorn in the flesh, which came from Paul's enemy, somehow turned out to be his friend. What Satan intended to trouble and annoy Paul turned out for his good because it kept him from the sins of pride and arrogance.

This teaches us four helpful lessons:

1. God uses the work of our enemies to serve His purposes, even to keep us from sin.

2. Pain and suffering from any source weakens us, and we may repeatedly cry out to God to remove it or change it. But God's power is made perfect in our weakness.

3. When God does not remove our thorn, He will send sufficient grace to enable us to bear it.

4. God's grace makes us strong even when we are weak. What a blessed mystery.

The blind Scottish preacher George Matheson (1842–1906) wrote these beautiful words as a prayer:

> I have thanked Thee a thousand times for my roses, but never once for my "thorn"…teach me the glory of my cross; teach me the value of my "thorn"! Show me that I have climbed to Thee by the path of pain. Show me that my tears have become my rainbow.

As women we must learn how to depend on God's grace for strength. We need to see God in our thorns and let Him turn our trials into beneficial steppingstones. With Paul we can say, "Therefore I will boast all the more gladly of my weaknesses, so that the power of Christ may rest upon me" (2 Corinthians 12:9).

It's not about us; it's about Him. Let us return often to the promise in Hebrews 4:16 that when we draw near to the throne of grace with confidence, we will find mercy and grace to help in our time of need.

God uses wounded, imperfect people to accomplish His divine purposes. None of us are worthy of His grace. God's love and care for women is so encompassing that it covers the most degrading sins that have been done against them and by them. The genealogy of Jesus Christ in Matthew 1 includes four unlikely women by whom God chose to showcase His grace: Tamar, the daughter-in-law of Judah (Genesis 38); Rahab, the Canaanite prostitute (Joshua 2); Ruth, the pagan foreigner (Ruth 1–4); and Bathsheba, the wife of Uriah (2 Samuel 11).

Incest. Prostitution. Idolatry. Adultery. These sins were not a hindrance to God who chose these women to demonstrate that no one is too sinful or too broken to receive His forgiveness and blessing. Oh, what encouragement and hope!

Finally, we are told to grow in the grace and knowledge of our Lord and Savior Jesus Christ (2 Peter 3:18). In His love, God will provide circumstances in which we'll need His grace. That is how we grow in grace. In our desperation for relief from the pain of our thorns, we will become more acquainted with the extent and value of God's grace. Otherwise, how would we ever know how wonderful and sufficient His grace is unless we needed it?

Here is a practical reminder of what grace looks like in our lives:

Growing, not perfect

Responsible for my choices and actions

Attitudes in suffering are pleasing to God

Capacity to love and serve others is increasing

Extending God's grace to others

God's grace is our salvation, our help, and our strength. We *experience* grace when we become God's daughters. We *live* in grace to receive daily strength so that we can suffer well and be obedient to His word. Let us *extend* gentle grace to others—undeserved kindness and mercy—as it has been given to us.

Taking God's Word to Heart

1. What is the grace of God? Why do we need it?

2. How do we know when we experience God's grace? List the many ways God shows us His grace from Ephesians 1 and 2.

3. Describe the relationship between grace and works in Ephesians 2:8-9.

4. Give an example of how you have shown grace to someone when they didn't deserve it. How did that experience help you to understand God's grace to you?

Philippians 3:13-14—*Forgetting what lies behind and straining forward to what lies ahead; I press on toward the goal for the prize of the upward call of God in Christ Jesus.*

1 Corinthians 15:58 (NIV)—*Therefore, my dear brothers and sisters, stand firm. Let nothing move you. Always give yourselves fully to the work of the Lord, because you know that your labor in the Lord is not in vain.*

Romans 8:28—*And we know that for those who love God all things work together for good, for those who are called according to his purpose.*

God's grace has watched over and followed me all my life. I wouldn't be where I am today without it. On July 25, 1947, a baby girl was born to a couple living in a trailer on the campus of Dallas Theological Seminary, joining her big brother. My father was in the US Navy and my mother in the Air Force when they were introduced by a mutual friend, and they married in 1945 just months before the end of World War II. Weary of the war and military service, they were anxious to settle down and start a family.

They were both young Christians (Mother had just left the Reorganized Church of the Latter-day Saints, a branch of Mormonism) and growing in their faith and knowledge of the Bible. But from the beginning of their marriage they experienced great marital conflict. They both had unrealistic and unusual expectations, and together came up with some unconventional methods of punishment that would leave their children with emotional and spiritual wounds.

Vastly different backgrounds and painful events in their lives and memories of the Depression left them ill-prepared for the challenges of marriage and parenting. Within eight years, four more children joined the family. When I was ten, my family of eight moved into a partially finished structure one-half mile off the highway by a dirt road. Though it was 1956, this "house" did not have a flushing toilet or telephone. The only furniture was a kitchen table and chairs and beds—mostly old metal army cots. The only appliances were a refrigerator, a cooking stove, one small heating stove, and a washing machine that drained into one side of a divided utility tub. The other side served as a kitchen sink. The roof leaked in several places, so twenty-gallon metal cans stood in place to catch the dripping water when it rained. This forty-by-forty-foot shack had just one dividing wall. Boxes of clothes, books, and junk created small spaces that became "rooms." Prior to this move, we had lived in a variety of locations, enduring hardship and poverty.

Anger and regret fueled heated arguments. Though my father had attended a seminary program, hoping to go into full-time ministry, marital conflict and my mother's multiple health problems had prevented this. She was emotionally and physically unable to take care of six children and the household.

Trying to cope with these difficult circumstances, my parents inflicted severe emotional and physical discipline and punishment on their six children for both real and imagined disobedience. Cruel words and actions wounded our spirits and bodies. I often wondered why I had been born into this family. Poverty, neglect, and abuse produced shame and humiliation in all of us. At times I wore certain clothes in order to hide strap marks on my arms and legs.

At school, I felt so different from my classmates; I had no pretty clothes or nice shoes to wear, just hand-me-downs from my older brother or secondhand clothes from Goodwill. But my one redeeming quality was that I was smart and could help others with their homework and study questions.

As the oldest daughter, it was my responsibility to cook and wash dishes. There were also endless loads of laundry to wash, hang out to dry, and later fold. Sometimes I even had to care for livestock. I was called upon to take care of my younger brothers and sisters and even had to take care of my mother when she was sick. There was no time for studying as I fell into bed exhausted each night. Schoolwork had to wait until the early morning hours, when my father woke me to iron his shirt before he left for work. Sometimes I was fortunate enough to get an uninterrupted hour in which I could study and do homework before walking a mile and a half to school. Occasionally, I made it to the highway to ride the school bus.

Strangely, in this harsh atmosphere, my parents loved God and taught us to revere and love the Bible. At times, we were required to sit quietly and listen to various radio Bible teachers. At Christmastime, we always listened to the entire *Messiah* on an old reel-to-reel tape recorder. Our family attended a small Bible church, and in the summer, we kids loved going to a Christian camp in another state. But no one could have imagined what was going on inside our home. It was a sad and dark secret.

My life as a teenager was burdened and isolated. I knew that life should be different than it was. In spite of this, I grew up with a desire and longing to know God. I had accepted Christ as my Savior at the age of seven and wanted to be a missionary nurse. Sometimes I slipped from my cot at night and read my Bible by the pilot light of the water heater. I was sustained by the belief that God really did love me and that He had a plan for my life. I always had the hope that there was something better out there, and that I must survive in order to find it.

It was from this environment that I left to attend Bible college in the midsixties, hoping to fulfill my long-term dream of becoming a missionary nurse. For as long as I could remember, I had wanted to be a nurse. Although very young, I had been deeply affected by the news of the five martyred missionaries in Ecuador in 1955. It was always with this desire, and God's claim on my life, that I pursued a missions major in Bible college and spent time in a missionary internship in Central America and Mexico in 1968. But God had a different plan for me, and three months after graduating in 1969, I married a promising young professor and preacher, Erwin Wesley Lutzer, whom I had met in a church during his years at Dallas Seminary. When it later became apparent that I would become a pastor's wife, I thought God had made a mistake—this was the one thing I had told God I never wanted to be.

More than you can ever imagine, I was unprepared for this role. I had never seen my mother entertain or practice hospitality. She had no dining or living room furniture. No china, silverware, lovely furnishings, or beautiful pictures on the wall. How would I know what to do as a pastor's wife? God was asking me to do the impossible. I was shy, scared, and felt inferior to the women in our first church. No one knew of my background. God was challenging me to overcome these obstacles and learn how to be hospitable and show grace and kindness to others.

When we were invited to someone's home for dinner, I would take mental notes on how to set the table, what to serve, and how to serve it. I was awed by the beautiful homes and furnishings of our parishioners. I once told my husband that if I had a thousand dollars, I wouldn't even know what to buy to make our home look lovely.

As time passed, however, I began to gain confidence, though I was worried and anxious about preparing for and serving our guests. With small children to care for and a busy husband, I had no one to help me. I fretted and often felt under enormous stress. What would people think about my home and my presentation? How could I possibly serve them with the same grace and ability they had served us with? I knew that it didn't really matter what they thought, as my ministry of hospitality should be done for the Lord, but I was still nervous and apprehensive.

Over the years, sweet friends have helped and encouraged me to gain the confidence needed to practice and hone my skills. I've come to realize that the state of my heart is far more important than the state of my home, though there is correlation between the two and one affects the other.

As the years passed, my greatest joy has been in being a mother. My three daughters, Lorisa Beth, Lynette Marie, and Lisa Christine, are very precious to me and we had wonderful, happy years together as they grew up into beautiful young women who love the Lord. They are now all married to wonderful men and have given us eight delightful grandchildren.

At the age of forty, I sensed a midlife crisis coming on. I was feeling very negative about myself, and I earnestly sought the Lord. Since my mother's death in December 1985, I had experienced much inner turmoil, anger, discouragement, and dissatisfaction with my life. I began to recall many of the horrible events of my childhood, and I realized that I had picked up some sinful, negative attitudes that were now affecting my relationship with my husband and children.

God began to deal severely with me, allowing me to go through many months of darkness, doubt, and soul-searching. He loved me so much that He could not allow me to continue to live with a rebellious and stubborn heart. Thus began a period of quiet despair, depression, deep loneliness, and spiritual oppression. It seemed as though God had put me on a shelf and said, "I can't use you until you surrender and are broken." I had great anguish of spirit as God broke me, and I came to the place where I acknowledged God's sovereign control over my life.

Sometimes I lay facedown on the floor as I wept and wrestled with God over my sin and the sin that had been done to me. I often read the Psalms and in brokenness asked for God's merciful forgiveness and cleansing. No one knew what I was going through, not even my husband. On Sundays it was agonizing to sit in church, hold my head up, and be a kind and friendly pastor's wife. I wanted to disappear and hide; surely everyone could see my agony.

Slowly my senses returned, and God began to heal and restore. I felt like a new person and eagerly sought the Lord's will. I asked God one more time, *Is it in Your will for me to ever become a nurse?* It was as though I heard His voice say, "Yes, now is the time. You may begin."

Voices of doubt filled my mind: "You're too old. You'll never make it! You're not smart enough. Your brain is dead. What will people say?" But with joy, wonder, and great determination, I began taking the required courses in the late 1980s. I studied algebra, chemistry, microbiology, anatomy and physiology, and all the nursing courses. My husband and daughters encouraged me, supported me, and cheered me on. The night I graduated from nursing school was the most exciting one of my life. By God's merciful grace, I passed the state boards and went on to specialize in surgical nursing. Over the years God gave me many opportunities to comfort the sick and dying, to pray with patients and families, and to hold suffering, hurting people in my arms.

My life hasn't gone as I thought it would, but so much more has been given and so much more received than I could have ever imagined. Erwin and I wouldn't have chosen some of the experiences God had in mind for us, especially those involving pain and tragedy. However, He has worked all of these things together for good in our lives, and He always knows what's best. His grace has been sufficient over and over again in our lives and the lives of our daughters and their families.

Dear ladies, I can tell you without hesitation that my life is a picture of the grace of God. I have needed God's grace from the moment I was born—from an abusive, dysfunctional, tumultuous childhood... through lonely, sad teenage years...through hopeful, struggling Bible college years...through the happy and challenging years of marriage... through the sweet and exhausting years of motherhood...through my times of stubbornness, pride, anger, and resistance to God's will... through sickness, pain, and surgery...through years of ministering to and caring for others...in these joyful years of grandmotherhood—right up to this very moment. I have needed God's amazing grace throughout my life, and He has poured out His grace to me in abundance. "But by the grace of God I am what I am, and his grace toward me was not in vain" (1 Corinthians 15:10).

> Through many dangers, toils, and snares,
> I have already come.
> 'Tis grace hath brought me safe thus far,
> And grace will lead me home.

Taking God's Word to Heart

Take as much time as you need to write out your life story and how God's grace kept, protected, changed, disciplined, and blessed you all along the way. Be honest as you write about your sin, suffering, sorrow, success, and salvation.

INTEGRITY

Psalm 7:8—*Judge me, O L*ORD*,*
according to my righteousness
and according to the integrity that is in me.

Psalm 25:21—
May integrity and uprightness preserve me,
for I wait for you.

Proverbs 2:7—*He stores up sound wisdom for the upright;*
he is a shield to those who walk in integrity.

I know a woman who confessed she was misleading her husband by doctoring their checkbook. She was spending more than the amounts she entered in the check register, but she also knew that this cheating would catch up with her. She could fool her husband, but she could not fool the bank, and the humiliating truth had to be told.

Perhaps she is an extreme example, but dishonesty of one kind or another is found everywhere: within families, in the workplace, among friends, and in everyday relationships. We complain that integrity is lacking among our politicians, in serious governmental and international relationships, in financial institutions, in businesses, in the courts and judicial system, in the medical field and pharmaceutical companies. But we have to look no further than our own hearts to find the seeds of dishonesty. Apparently, integrity is something we require of others but not necessarily of ourselves. People who firmly adhere to a code of moral values are becoming scarce.

There are many uses of *integrity* or its synonyms in Scripture. The most outstanding man of integrity is Job. Even after his children, servants, and animals had been killed, we read that God said to Satan, "Have you considered my servant Job, that there is none like him on the earth, a blameless and upright man, who fears God and turns away from evil? He still holds fast his *integrity* although you incited me against him to destroy him without reason" (Job 2:3, italics added).

Jesus was recognized, even by those who despised Him, as One who had integrity. When the Pharisees sent disciples to trap Him, they began by saying, "Teacher, we know that you are true and teach the way of God truthfully, and you do not care about anyone's opinion, for you are not swayed by appearances" (Matthew 22:16). Jesus both *spoke* the truth and *was* the truth.

Integrity means virtue, honesty, truth, honor, reliability, and uprightness. The importance of virtue is emphasized in 2 Peter 1:5-7 (italics added) where the eight qualities of Christian character are listed: "For this very reason, make every effort to supplement your *faith* with *virtue*, and virtue with *knowledge*, and knowledge with *self-control*, and self-control with *steadfastness*, and steadfastness with *godliness*, and godliness with *brotherly affection*, and brotherly affection with *love*."

It is clear that integrity defines the essence of one's character; it makes us into a wholly integrated person. God uses our integrity to accomplish His work within us:

- He evaluates us according to our integrity (Psalm 7:8).
- He is a shield to those who walk in it (Proverbs 2:7).
- Integrity increases our intimate fellowship with Him (Psalm 15).
- Integrity preserves us (Psalm 25:21).
- Integrity matures us to be a productive and fruitful Christian (2 Peter 1:8).

D.L. Moody said that character is what a person is in the dark.

Unfortunately, our generation finds it difficult to distinguish character from reputation. But actually our character is more important and cannot be damaged. How should we behave when someone tries to harm our reputation? The Scripture instructs us this way, "When reviled, we bless; when persecuted, we endure; when slandered, we entreat" (1 Corinthians 4:12-13). In the face of slander and belittling words in the workplace or any place, the Bible says that "the integrity of the upright guides them" (Proverbs 11:3). Our responsibility is to continue being an honest and dependable person no matter what is said about us.

Integrity lies at the heart of strong, healthy families. It has been said that, "Every father and mother should remember that one day their son or daughter will follow their example instead of their advice." As mothers, we must set the bar for honesty for our children. We will teach them that copying the work of others and cheating are wrong, and we will call them on it. We will not lie to cover our child's tardiness or absence at school. We will not lie to a caller as to why we can't say yes to their request. We will not lie to cover a mistake or to make ourselves look better in a difficult situation. We will not lie about why we are late to work or to a meeting. We will not lie to a relative as to why we can't visit them. Integrity means we speak the truth even if it costs us personally. We must tell the truth even if we are embarrassed, fear that we'll be rejected, or get into some kind of trouble.

It is always best to tell the truth and trust God to help us navigate through the consequences. Perhaps we need to learn how to be on time for work and appointments through better time management and planning ahead—and to teach our children to do the same. Everyone has relatives who are difficult to be with, so think ahead how you will respond to an invitation gracefully and truthfully.

We've all been tempted to lie about something at some time. We've all had lapses in integrity when we failed miserably. Our sin nature, our thoughts and desires, and the devil himself can lead us to protect ourselves by lying. The devil is the biggest liar of all, and the Bible tells us that he is the father of lies (John 8:44). The devil is our enemy and wants us to be more like him than like Jesus. We are never more like the devil than when we lie. He can influence our minds and thoughts to lie about anything and everything. He can even use other people to ask us to lie and cover for them.

When we have compromised our integrity, God enables us to recover from our mistakes. Women of integrity can then speak the truth even though it may be costly to them personally. We may have to confess to telling a lie to save our necks or prevent embarrassing ourselves. Our confession of sin should be as broad as the offense itself. If we have sinned against our husbands, we must confess to them; if we have lied to our children, a friend, or an employer, we have to admit to it. We must remember,

> Whoever conceals their sins does not prosper,
>   but the one who confesses and renounces them finds
>   mercy.
>   (Proverbs 28:13 NIV)

Perhaps you are tempted to lie often—or at least stretch the truth to make yourself look better. Here is a remedy that is guaranteed to work: Every time you tell someone a lie or stretch the truth, pause and then immediately admit, "I just lied to you. Please forgive me." You will not need to go through this very many times before you realize how sinful it is to lie and that you want to always speak the truth. A helpful prayer is this,

> Deliver me, O LORD,
>   from lying lips,
>   from a deceitful tongue.
>   (Psalm 120:2)

Restoring integrity begins with repentance and thoroughly, honestly examining our hearts in God's presence. We must be willing to do anything to be fully right with God and others. To quote the words of Job, "Let me be weighed in a just balance, and let God know my integrity!" (Job 31:6).

Psalm 15:2-5 provides for us the characteristics of a person of integrity:

- Do what is right and speak the truth first to ourselves in our own hearts (v. 2).

- Honor others (friends and enemies) by refusing to speak slander, gossip, or rumors about them (v. 3).

- Keep our word even when it hurts. We keep and honor our sacred oath of marriage even when it is difficult and lonely. We keep our promises and the secrets that have been entrusted to us (v. 4).

- Refuse to take advantage of others. We wisely lend money without asking for interest. We refuse to take bribes, and are fair and honest in our business dealings. We do not defraud those who work for us. Our word is our bond (v. 5).

I heard Stuart Briscoe tell the story of when he worked in a bank in England and the manager wanted him to do something dishonest, the equivalent of cheating the customers. Stuart's response was, "If you want me to steal *for* you, what makes you think I might not also steal *from* you?" Exactly.

Some principles are worth being fired for; some virtues are worth losing your inheritance for; some moral convictions are worth going to jail for; some standards are worth failing college for.

Let us remember that integrity is fragile. Once we have lost it, it takes time to get it back. In some cases, we may never get it back. Integrity is like a valuable vase on a mantel that falls to the floor and must be glued back together. Even after we have carefully fitted and glued the pieces in place, the hairline cracks show where the breaks were.

Let us call on God, asking Him to give us both the desire and the ability to be people of truth in our decaying society. To strengthen our integrity with the Word of God, we can pray this prayer every day:

> Let the words of my mouth and the meditation of
>   my heart
>   be acceptable in your sight,
>   O LORD, my rock and my redeemer.
> (Psalm 19:14)

Taking God's Word to Heart

1. Where does integrity originate? Why is it so important for us to maintain it?

2. How does the lack of integrity affect our character?

3. What can you do to strengthen your integrity?

LOVING GOD

Deuteronomy 10:12-13—*"And now, Israel, what does the* LORD *your God require of you, but to fear the* LORD *your God, to walk in all his ways, to love him, to serve the* LORD *your God with all your heart and with all your soul, and to keep the commandments and statutes of the* LORD, *which I am commanding you today for your good?"*

Mark 12:30—*"You shall love the Lord your God with all your heart and with all your soul and with all your mind and with all your strength."*

1 John 4:19—*We love because he first loved us.*

The commandment to love the Lord our God is so exhaustive, so complete and demanding, that it seems impossible for a human being to do. Though I greatly desire to do so, I fall short of fulfilling this command in every area. What does such a love for God really mean?

As I pondered these Scripture verses found both in the Old and the New Testaments, three questions immediately came to mind. First, who could possibly love God like this? My heart is often preoccupied and subdued toward God. The demands of my life press against my clock and calendar, asking for more of my soul, mind, and strength. I'm guilty of giving God what is left rather than *all* of it as He demands.

Second, is it possible to love an invisible being with so much passion? I find it difficult to love God as I ought to when I hear the endless stories of misery, killing, abuse, poverty, and evil in the world. If God doesn't intervene when He has the power to do so, I sometimes wonder if He really cares about the suffering and pain on this earth. God is so great and holy that for me to love Him as He has commanded involves mystery and unanswered questions.

Third, if I loved God with all my heart, soul, mind, and strength, would I have enough love left over for anyone else? Even though I love my husband dearly, perhaps I don't love him as I ought to. Loving our family, friends, neighbors, and even our enemies, as we're also commanded to do, could leave us feeling drained and empty.

However, honestly—deep within my heart and soul—a part of me desperately wants to love God just as He wants me to. The words of David in the Psalms capture the essence of what God is asking us to do:

> As a deer pants for flowing streams,
>   so pants my soul for you, O God.
>   (Psalm 42:1)

Yes, I do want to love God with all that I am, as a thirsty deer longs for water, and I suspect you do also.

"You shall love the Lord your God with all your heart and with all your soul and with all your mind and with all your strength" (Mark 12:30). Let's look at each phrase in this commandment Jesus gave us to discover what it means.

To love God *with all our heart* means that we must feel deeply toward Him with a sense of awe, reverence, and respect for who He is and what He has done for us in Christ (Ephesians 1). It means that we defend His name and reputation in the world. When we hear someone use God's name as a swear word, our hearts will be grieved. Many people will make up their mind about God based upon the way we live and behave. Those who say they are Christ-followers, and yet live just like their unsaved friends, are living a testimony unworthy of the gospel.

Joseph could have rationalized having sex with Potiphar's wife when she tried to seduce him. But Joseph was more concerned about God's reputation and desires than he was his own. He understood that sexual immorality was a serious offense against God and said, "How then can I do this great wickedness and sin against God?" (Genesis 39:9). If we love God with all our heart, we will not grieve and insult Him by living immorally (1 John 5:1-3).

God was very angry with His people Israel when they worshipped other gods—counterfeit gods made of wood and stone, weak and powerless, though energized by Satan and evil spirits. As the only holy, supreme God of the universe, He commanded, "You shall have no other gods before me" (Exodus 20:3). If our affections and attention are greater for a person or a circumstance than they are for God, we too can be guilty of the sin of idolatry.

To love God *with all our soul* means that we choose to love Him with a purpose. We must make a choice to prefer Him above others—to long for His fellowship, presence, and joy:

> You make known to me the path of life;
>   in your presence there is fullness of joy;
>   at your right hand are pleasures forevermore.
> (Psalm 16:11)

God will test our loyalty by asking us to make some tough choices in His favor. That's what He did with Abraham when He asked him to take his son Isaac and offer him up as a burnt offering on Mt. Moriah (Genesis 22:1-14). However incomprehensible and excruciating this request was, Abraham obeyed God, and just as he lifted the knife to kill his son, God stopped him: "Because you have done this and have not withheld your son, your only son, I will surely bless you" (22:16-17). We can't say that we love God with all our soul unless we are willing to sacrifice for Him.

God may ask us to give up someone or something we love and cherish deeply to test our love and loyalty to Him. Often He will ask us to give up lesser things, such as time, money, jobs, pleasure, health, convenience, sports, entertainment, or possessions, to prove that we are willing to sacrifice for Him. It doesn't mean that we don't love our spouses, children, family, and friends, but that we love Him *more*.

To love God *with all our mind* means that we should be able to think clearly, deeply, and often about God. This is a difficult assignment because we are bombarded with noises and moving images from multiple media sources. Our minds are filled with thoughts of trivia, romance, food, and things we want. Is there any time left to contemplate Almighty God? It is another form of idolatry to think bigger thoughts about everything else than we think about God.

We cannot love God with all of our mind unless we meditate on His Word so that we might think His thoughts about Him. Now there's a unique thought. If you don't know what to think about God or what to say to Him, read Psalm 145:1-5 aloud to Him: "I will extol you, my God and King, and bless your name forever and ever…"

Loving God with all our minds is to worship Him by singing songs and hymns and praying prayers of adoration. Do you fall asleep thanking Him for the care and sustaining strength He gave you for that day?

> My eyes are awake before the watches of the night,
>> that I may meditate on your promise.
>> (Psalm 119:148)

Do you wake up thanking Him for the night of rest and asking Him for grace and mercy for the new day?

> I lay down and slept;
>> I woke again, for the LORD sustained me.
>> (Psalm 3:5)

I have made a habit of doing this, and encourage you to do the same.

To love God *with all our strength* means that we discipline our heart, soul, and mind to accomplish the greatest task of all, that of seeking Him. Hebrews 11:6 tells us that God rewards those who seek Him. We must jealously guard our time of prayer, fellowship, and Bible reading and study. Prepare yourself, make a plan, and do it enough times until it becomes a habit. We can give Him the best part of our day when our minds are fresh and our strength has been renewed.

Keeping the greatest commandment means that we will love what God loves: His Son Jesus, His Word, His people, and Himself. Psalms 45:7 tells us, "you have loved righteousness and hated wickedness." We must also hate what God hates—sin in every form that breaks His commandments and dishonors Him.

How strange and sad that we often love what God hates and hate what God loves. In 1 John 2:15 we are told that we should not love the world, for if any one loves the world "the love of the Father is not in him." We can prove that we love the Father by not loving the world system of evil, greed, immorality, and pleasure.

Matt Chandler summarizes so well how passionate we should be in our pursuit of God:

> Instead of pursuing him with steadfast passion and enthralled fury—instead of loving him with all our heart, soul, mind, and strength; instead of attributing to him glory and honor and praise and power and wisdom and strength—we just try to take his toys and run. It is still idolatry to want God for his benefits but not for himself.

Finally, Jesus expands on the first and greatest commandment by saying, "And a second is like it: You shall love your neighbor as yourself" (Matthew 22:39). Another demanding, seemingly impossible command. It is another test of our love for God: "Whoever claims to love God yet hates a brother or sister is a liar. For whoever does not love their brother and sister, whom they have seen, cannot love God, whom they have not seen" (1 John 4:20). There is a fundamental incompatibility between a passionate love for God and hatred for a fellow human being. Loving God will enable us to love others.

I'm reminded of the story of a four-year-old girl named Evie who had one arm around one doll and the other arm around a second doll, and said to her mother, "Mommy, I love them and I love them and I love them, but they never love me back!" Since God has loved us so much in Jesus Christ, loving Him back should be our first priority. "We love Him because He first loved us" (1 John 4:19 NKJV).

Taking God's Word to Heart

1. Read Ephesians 1. Then take an hour to just think about God's love for us—His greatness, awesomeness, and the plan of redemption He provided for us.

2. What things does God hate as described in Proverbs 6:16-19?

3. How can we show God that we love Him with all of our heart, soul, mind, and body?

4. What changes will you make to show God that you love Him in this way?

MODESTY

Proverbs 11:22—*Like a gold ring in a pig's snout is a beautiful woman without discretion.*

1 Corinthians 6:19-20—*Or do you not know that your body is a temple of the Holy Spirit within you, whom you have from God? You are not your own, for you were bought with a price. So glorify God in your body.*

1 Peter 3:4—*But let your adorning be the hidden person of the heart with the imperishable beauty of a gentle and quiet spirit, which in God's sight is very precious.*

A few years ago, a well-endowed young woman wearing a tiny bikini and accompanied by a couple of guys entered the store where I was shopping. Every eye stared in astonishment. Her almost naked body was distracting to everyone. We happened to meet in the greeting card section. As I tried to concentrate on choosing some cards, a mother with a couple of preteen boys stepped into the aisle and gasped, and then quickly moved her sons on to the next aisle.

I turned to the gal and said, "I think your behavior is offending people. Could you please go and put some clothes on?"

She was surprised that I would speak to her, and laughing, she turned to her friends and said, "Let's get out of here." A few minutes later, she reappeared and loudly said, "Hey lady, I'm offended by what you said to me. You just need to get over it." With that, she quickly exited the store.

What has happened to modesty? Where has the sense of personal privacy and decency gone? *Modesty* has a number of meanings: decency (avoiding indecency), propriety, moderation, decorum, restraint, discretion, humility, dignity, appropriateness, deference, freedom from vanity or conceit, and a form of self-control.

I am appalled and annoyed at the number of women on television—reporters, anchors, analysts, contributors, performers, celebrities, and those being interviewed—with plunging necklines and short skirts. I feel uncomfortable for them. If it is distracting to me as a woman, it must be very distracting to the men who are watching.

In many public places, I see women whose outfits resemble bedtime attire rather than daytime clothing. Often I'm tempted to ask, "Excuse me, did you forget to get dressed this morning?" I wonder why they think everyone wants to see their bodies. The general public is forced to look at nearly bare breasts. It seems that women who have the most, flaunt the most. It's as if they're shouting, "Look at me!"

Does our feminine need to be admired and desired overwhelm our sense of decency and moderation? Being sexy so that we'll be noticed first and often seems to be all that matters anymore. And the competition is fierce. Wanting to be fashionable, even Christian women show their cleavage at weddings and other social events. Is the old excuse legitimate that women can't find any modest clothing to buy—that the fashion industry designs only immodest and sexy styles? Have we succumbed to the worldly mindset that it is normal and acceptable to show as much as possible and not cross the line of being inappropriate?

Sue Edwards, associate professor of educational ministries and leadership at Dallas Theological Seminary, wrote,

> I wonder if these women realize how much their insensitivity hurts our chances of being taken seriously by men. Seems to me when we show cleavage, we back up what men have said and thought about women for centuries. We care more about the power of our sexuality than we do about its effect on our brothers. We aren't thinking about

the long-term impact of our choices, just about how cute we look today. Or maybe it's too much trouble for busy women to assess the effect of the gap. That's understandable for immature women who don't know better. But not for leaders with far-reaching influence. [20]

Women need to stop whining about men lacking self-control and lusting after them when they see cleavage. Men are wired to look at and admire breasts—it's in their DNA. Good and godly men who want to be faithful to their wives are tempted to have a second look. In fact, it's impossible not to look when it's in your face everywhere.

In her book *Glittering Vices*, Rebecca DeYoung warns us not to confuse sexual desire with lust. She defines lust as a "reductive impulse" directed toward "one's own individual gratification, apart from a relationship to a person." [21] Sexual desire is God-given and not sinful. It turns into lust and becomes sinful when it is acted upon either by mental imagination or by a physical act. But the way many women dress tempts men to move from what is normal interest to what is truly lustful.

In the name of beauty and fashion, many Christian women dress in a provocative way. We have equated being beautiful with being sexy and showing as much skin as we dare. "Somehow we must find the root cause and help women uncover the reason for the gap in their personal thinking and actions." [22] We must take the time to consider why we put clothes on in the first place.

When God created Adam and Eve, why do you suppose they were naked and unashamed before each other and before God? Was it because God created their bodies in exact proportion to their height and weight, a BMI of 20, and with perfect curves and bulges? Stacie Parlee-Johnson gives us the answer.

> True nakedness in this account is more than a mere physical condition. It indicates a right relationship with God, which includes both the physical and spiritual state. Adam and Eve covered themselves because the covenant with

God and with one another was broken. The direct correlation between disobedience and rebellion is shame in
nakedness and the putting on of *clothing*. [23]

Nancy Leigh DeMoss observes that "from this point on in the Bible,
nakedness (outside of marriage) is referred to as shameful." [24]

Adam and Eve's covering of fig leaves was inadequate, but God in
mercy performed the first animal sacrifice and made garments of skin
for them to wear. Blood was shed to obtain an acceptable covering for
their nakedness. Clothing is a gift from God covering our nakedness
and shame. [25]

Parlee-Johnson goes on to explain what the second Adam (Jesus
Christ) did for us in dying on the cross (1 Corinthians 15:45-49). When
Jesus was crucified, soldiers removed His clothing, leaving Him naked
as He hung there before the world in shame. Do you understand the
parallel? Christ cancelled Adam and Eve's sin when He took on the
shame and nakedness of the human race. He became sin for us; Christ
became our righteous clothing. [26]

The New Testament teaches us that our Savior is a covering for our
sin and protects us from sinning: "But put on the Lord Jesus Christ,
and make no provision for the flesh, to gratify its desires" (Romans
13:14). It is theologically correct to say that as believers we are to put on
Christ Himself as our righteous clothing. "Christ clothes us [with His
righteousness] at conversion, will continue to clothe us as we are sanc-
tified, and at the time of righteous judgment, we will be seen through
Christ in us, through our wearing of Christ. The need for clothing is a
confession of our need for Christ Himself." [27]

Going back to Adam and Eve once again, we can now understand
that nakedness was intended by God to be sacred between one man
and one woman in marriage. Clothing our bodies allows us to protect
what belongs to us and to our husbands from the eyes of others. When
sin entered the human race, everything changed. The sin nature drives
our desire to show our nakedness to "try to control and exploit men,

and even other women, to placate our selfish desires." [28] Normal sexual desire can easily turn into lust and evil. Physical beauty is a form of power, and women use it to seduce and to control just about anyone and anything.

True modesty will come only from a holy relationship with Jesus Christ, not as a vestige left over from the Victorian era. Jo March and her sisters in *Little Women* dressed modestly in contrast to how Elizabeth Bennet and her sisters dressed in *Pride and Prejudice*. There was more cleavage at one of those high-society balls than there is at most high-school proms today. [29]

In our desire to be culturally relevant, we have allowed *Vogue* and *Elle*, celebrities, and our peers to set the standard for us. We've forgotten who we are as women redeemed by Christ. Jesus has everything to do with what we put on and what we take off. Teach your daughter why she should be modest and set an example for her. As dedicated Christ-followers, we can begin a new trend and set the style for others to follow.

Parlee-Johnson's concluding words both convict and embolden us to be women of modesty, restraint, discretion, dignity, and self-control.

> The world tells us to throw off our clothing and to not be ashamed of our nakedness, to revel in womanhood and its potential power. And perhaps, by comparison to most of the women you see, you feel you're doing well. But we don't need this power the world *seduces us* with. We don't need any other power but what is found in Jesus Christ. We are now in Christ, and we put Him on. We are not clothed with the "treasures" that this world affords. The confidence in Christ that we have does not give us license to showcase pieces of ourselves that were made for intimacy and union in sacred places. So to the world, confess who you are in Christ by showing who you are without Him—naked and ashamed. [30]

Muhammad Ali is alleged to have said these words to his daughter:

> Everything that God made valuable in the world is cov-
> ered and hard to get to. Where do you find diamonds?
> Deep down in the ground, covered and protected. Where
> do you find pearls? Deep down at the bottom of the ocean,
> covered up and protected in a beautiful shell. Where do
> you find gold? Way down in the mine, covered over with
> layers and layers of rock. Where do you find oil? Deep in
> the earth compressed under rock and shale. You've got to
> work hard to get to them. Your body is sacred. You're far
> more precious than diamonds and pearls, and you should
> be covered too. [31]

Now we know what modesty is:

> a wall to the uninvited,
> a guardian to what is protected,
> an invitation to the respectful,
> a statement of values to the unbeliever,
> a sense of dignity to the culture that wages war on our
> worth,
> and a gift of honor to the One we represent. [32]

Taking God's Word to Heart

1. Upon what foundation is modesty based? Where does it originate?

2. Explain why Adam and Eve were ashamed of their nakedness
   after they sinned.

3. How will what you have learned about modesty affect your
   thinking and the way you dress?

PRAYER

Psalm 86:6-7—*Give ear, O LORD, to my prayer;*
listen to my plea for grace.
In the day of my trouble I call upon you,
for you answer me.

Ephesians 6:16,18—*In all circumstances take up the*
shield of faith...praying at all times in the Spirit, with
all prayer and supplication. To that end keep alert with
all perseverance, making supplication for the saints.

1 Thessalonians 5:16-18—*Rejoice always, pray*
without ceasing, give thanks in all circumstances; for
this is the will of God in Christ Jesus for you.

The subject of prayer is inexhaustible, profound and yet simple. For centuries theologians have wrestled with what prayer is and isn't. There is not space enough in this short chapter to do it justice—the what, when, where, why, and how of it. The healthy and sick, rich and poor, scholars and simple, kings and queens and peasants, and everyone in between have prayed to Jehovah God, creator of heaven and earth.

From Abraham in Genesis to Moses, Hannah, David, Job, Isaiah, Mary, Jesus, Paul, Peter, and John in Revelation, theirs are the magnificent prayers of Scripture. All are worthy of our attention. But I am most intrigued, not by the prayers of men, but by the prayers of the divine One, Jesus. Why did *He* pray?

As we follow Him through the New Testament, questions arise: Why is it that Jesus, the Son of God, second person of the Trinity, spent so much time in prayer? What was He praying about and why did He pray? The Gospels give us a glimpse into His prayer life. When and where did Jesus pray?

On a mountain by Himself (Matthew 14:23); in the early morning darkness (Mark 1:35); in desolate places (Luke 5:16); all night on a mountain (Luke 6:12); alone and while with others (Luke 9:18); with and for His disciples and for us (John 17:6-10).

The answer to the question of why Jesus prayed so often and so much is that even though He was God, He lived as man—the God-man. He laid aside His heavenly glory, but He did not lay aside His divine attributes even though He chose not to use them. His miracles were done in dependence on the Father and His power. What does Jesus teach us about prayer?

He prayed continually: sometimes in the midst of performing a miracle, standing at the grave of Lazarus, before feeding the hungry multitude as He lifted the loaves and fish to heaven, after sending the disciples to the other side of the Sea of Galilee. He even prayed for His enemies as His physical life slowly ebbed away on the cross, "Father, forgive them, for they know not what they do" (Luke 23:34). Like a compass whose needle always points north, so Jesus, whether busy, resting or dying, was praying.

He prayed specifically. Listen to these words He prayed for Peter. "Simon, Simon, behold, Satan demanded to have you, that he might sift you like wheat, but I have prayed for you that your faith may not fail." Jesus tells Peter that He knows he will deny Him, but then assures Peter that he will be restored to fellowship and minister to others (Luke 22:31-32). In John 17, Jesus prays a powerful prayer of instruction and assurance for His disciples: "I do not ask that you take them out of the world, but that you keep them from the evil one" (17:15). This is a beautiful example of Jesus praying for those He loved—His disciples and those who would become His disciples—that they might face their own trials successfully.

Today, Jesus is seated at the right hand of His Father in heaven (Hebrews 10:12) and continues to pray for us, as it says in Hebrews 7:25, "since he always lives to make intercession for them."

He prayed submissively. Knowing that the cross was at hand, Jesus needed strength and assurance from His Father in order to be obedient to His Father's will. "Although he was a son, he learned obedience through what he suffered. And being made perfect, he became the source of eternal salvation to all who obey him" (Hebrews 5:8-9). One writer said, very correctly, "Jesus never found relief in His Divinity from His human suffering. He took refuge in prayer."

The same is true for us. If we genuinely long to be obedient to the Father's will, as Jesus was, then we must suffer. Our trials and suffering force us to agonize in prayer over the Father's will at the throne of grace, to be given mercy and grace to endure them successfully. The holiest path is not the smoothest path.

Jesus became acquainted with the rugged mountains of Judea and the wastelands near the Jordan River. He knew them well, as the text says, for He often slipped away to the mountain or into the wilderness to pray. It was there that He faced the first great test from His loving heavenly Father and the first great temptation from His mortal enemy Satan on the eve of beginning His ministry.

For us, what is the wilderness experience? God takes us to a place of isolation where there are no distractions except our human and spiritual needs—and God Himself. It is usually a place of loneliness, darkness, and conflict. I know this to be true because I have been there. There we are confronted with Him, the true and living God. There we are able to focus on what's in our hearts and our great need for God. We're able to get a clearer picture of our great sinfulness and His amazing love, forgiveness, and grace. The Word of God becomes intensely important as we seek to know Him more intimately.

We must also pray for one another. First Samuel 12:23 soberly reminds us, "far be it from me that I should sin against the Lord by ceasing to pray for you." Too often we get caught up in our own needs and trials and don't intercede for others. The bulk of the apostle Paul's prayer life was praying faithfully for others. In Ephesians 1:15-20 he wrote,

> For this reason, because I have heard of your faith in the Lord Jesus and your love toward all the saints, I do not cease to give thanks for you, remembering you in my prayers, that the God of our Lord Jesus Christ, the Father of glory, may give you the Spirit of wisdom and of revelation in the knowledge of him, having the eyes of your hearts enlightened, that you may know what is the hope to which he has called you, what are the riches of his glorious inheritance in the saints, and what is the immeasurable greatness of his power toward us who believe, according to the working of his great might that he worked in Christ when he raised him from the dead and seated him at his right hand in the heavenly places.

What a wonderful prayer to pray for anyone! "Prayer isn't the last thing—it's the *best thing* that you and I could ever do for anyone." [33]

Simply put, prayer is communication with God. Sometimes prayer is *listening* to God speak to us through His Word, as we read and meditate, asking Him to reveal Himself to us. Sometimes prayer is *talking* to God, telling Him our struggles, pain, anxieties, joy, confessing our sin and receiving His forgiveness—or just thanking Him for loving us and choosing us to be His child. God becomes the confidant, the friend who will understand perfectly and love us completely and unconditionally. Sometimes prayer is *something that cannot be uttered or heard.* [34] Romans 8:26 says, "Likewise the Spirit helps us in our weakness. For we do not know that to pray for as we ought, but the Spirit himself intercedes for us with groaning too deep for words."

When we are in severe emotional, spiritual, or physical pain, it may be virtually impossible for us to pray a coherent prayer. The Holy Spirit takes our groans, our screams, our tears, our muddled phrases, our anger and disappointment, and He transforms them into pure offerings. [35]

We pray because we must pray. R.A. Torrey, former president of Moody Bible Institute in Chicago, once wrote ten powerful reasons why believers should pray. Here are just a few of them:

- There is a devil and prayer is the God-appointed means of resisting him.

- Prayer with thanksgiving is the means of obtaining freedom from anxiety.

- Prayer is the means by which we are to keep watchful and be alert at Christ's return.

- Prayer is used by God to promote our spiritual growth, bring power into our work, lead others to faith in Christ, and bring all other blessings to Christ's church. [36]

I enjoy praying God's Word back to Him. The Bible says that God has elevated His Word above His name. God loves His Word. It is an expression of who He is. John 1:1 says, "In the beginning, was the Word, and the Word was with God, and the Word was God." Remind God of His promises, His love, His longsuffering and forgiveness. Praise and worship Him by reading the Psalms aloud.

I often use Ken Boa's *Handbook to Prayer*, a compilation of Scripture under the headings: Adoration, Confession, Renewal, Petition, Intercession, Affirmation, Thanksgiving, and Closing Prayer. Daily, I can pray God's Word back to Him in an organized manner. More than anything else, God wants us to know Him, to believe Him, to trust Him, to obey Him—no matter what.

One of my favorite verses is Hebrews 4:16, "Let us then with confidence draw near to the throne of grace, that we may receive mercy and find grace to help in time of need." This, I believe, is the secret to consistent praying. Let us confess our sin of unbelief and ask God for *confidence*, so that we may *draw near* (or pray). Draw near to what? The *throne of grace*—beautiful imagery—to receive *mercy* and find *grace* to help us in our time of need.

Oh, how we need to pray...because He prayed.

Taking God's Word to Heart

1. What is prayer? What is your greatest challenge in having a consistent prayer life?

2. Why did Jesus need to pray? How does His example help you see that prayer is a vital part of a Christian's life?

3. Why should we never allow "unanswered prayer" to be an excuse to stop praying? What is your plan to maintain a constant prayer life?

THE PRAYER OF OBEDIENCE

1 Samuel 15:22—
*"Behold, to obey is better than sacrifice,
and to listen than the fat of rams."*

Matthew 26:40-41— *"So, could you not
watch with me one hour? Watch and pray that
you may not enter into temptation. The spirit
indeed is willing, but the flesh is weak."*

Hebrews 5:7-8—*In the days of his flesh, Jesus offered
up prayers and supplications, with loud cries and tears,
to him who was able to save him from death, and he
was heard because of his reverence. Although he was a
son, he learned obedience through what he suffered.*

Jesus is a remarkable model of what obedience involves. The most dramatic example of this took place in Gethsemane, which was located on the Mount of Olives, so-called because of the many olive trees that grow there. In those days that area was mostly desert, and the olive trees provided a sheltered area that became known as the Garden of Gethsemane. After eating the last supper with His disciples in the upper room, Jesus went out with them and crossed the Kidron brook and entered this garden (John 18:1). This was one of Christ's favorite places, and He went there, as was His custom (Luke 22:39).

Come with me to witness His agony in this hallowed place. The magnificent and agonizing prayer of Jesus in Gethsemane takes us into the very throne room of heaven. Perhaps this is what is referred to in

Hebrews 4:16, "Let us then with confidence draw near to *the throne of grace*, that we may receive mercy and find grace to help in time of need" (italics added). Indeed, no greater mercy and grace has ever been given as was given to Christ in the Garden of Gethsemane.

The powers of darkness ringed around our Savior and attacked Him like a flock of vultures. Satan had already put it into the heart of Judas Iscariot to betray Him. But Jesus did not fear this, for He had declared earlier, "The ruler of this world is coming. He has no claim on me" (John 14:30).

In desperation Jesus asked if there might not be another way than the way of the cross. The impulse to escape from what He was about to endure overwhelmed Him. Satan is in the garden (much like his appearance in the Garden of Eden), not to kill Jesus but to offer again a way of escape just as he had done in the wilderness. He is tempting Jesus to avoid the cross and go directly to the crown. It was an escape route so that He would not become the sin bearer for mankind.

In His humanity, Jesus needed the companionship and support of His disciples and wanted them nearby during His suffering. But He was also concerned about *them* because they were confused, depressed, and exhausted. Jesus didn't hide His emotions; He honestly told them of the darkness and emotional trauma that was descending upon Him: "My soul is very sorrowful, even to death. Remain here and watch" (Mark 14:34). The horror of death on a cross, the torment of His accusers, the terror of bearing the sin of the world, and the separation from His Father on the cross caused Him to shrink back.

He was greatly distressed and troubled. His soul was sorrowful unto death. Being in agony He prayed more earnestly. He offered up prayers and supplications with loud cries and tears to Him who was able to save Him from death (Hebrews 5:7).

> And going a little farther he fell on his face and prayed, saying, "My Father, if it be possible, let this cup pass from me; nevertheless, not as I will, but as you will."...Again, for

the second time, he went away and prayed, "My Father, if this cannot pass unless I drink it, your will be done" (Matthew 26:39,42).

What is the meaning of the cup? It was the cup of iniquity to be drunk without a sedative; He would drink it full strength so that the price of our redemption might be purchased. He began to gaze into the cup of iniquity and discern its awful contents. He had gladly associated with sinners, but now He would be standing in the sinner's place, bearing the sinner's curse. "And there appeared to him an angel from heaven, strengthening him. And being in an agony he prayed more earnestly; and his sweat became like great drops of blood falling down to the ground" (Luke 22:43-44).

The darkness of Gethsemane foreshadowed the darkness of the cross. This cup was so overwhelming, it is described by various terms: perplexity, amazement, agony. "For our sake he made him to be sin who knew no sin, so that in him we might become the righteousness of God" (2 Corinthians 5:21). This was the antithesis to everything Jesus was—the Lamb without spot or blemish (1 Peter 1:19). Earlier He said, "For I tell you that this Scripture must be fulfilled in me: 'And he was numbered with the transgressors'" (Luke 22:37).

Finally, we see Christ's surrender and acceptance of the cup: "Nevertheless, not my will, but yours, be done" (Luke 22:42). In these eight words, Jesus gives His final answer to Satan and to the Father—"I will obey my Father; I will walk the torturous journey to the cross; I will drink the cup alone; I will shed My blood and the work of salvation will be finished."

Jesus didn't depend on His own abilities; He did not boast of His power. He didn't say, "O Father, I'm ready to go. I'm feeling strong tonight. I think I can crawl up on that cross and die and pull it off." *No*, He did not. On that dark night before His death—which had been planned before the foundation of the world—He prayed. He cried out to His Father to enable Him to be obedient to His last breath.

Someone has said, "During a test, the teacher is silent." Gethsemane was the test; Calvary was the answer. The victory of Calvary was won in Gethsemane through agonizing, powerful prayer. Our Lord Jesus Christ did not fail in His testing because He did not fail in His praying. He offered His will to the Father before He offered His life for us. He prayed before He faced His accusers, before He was beaten, before He was mocked, before the nails pierced His hands and feet, before He defeated Satan on the cross, and before He shed His precious blood to obtain our salvation.

Jesus confidently walked into the night of His betrayal and capture with composure because He had prayed, surrendered His will, and received grace and mercy. His focus was on the joy that would follow His obedience. Hebrews 12:2, says, "Looking to Jesus, the founder and perfecter of our faith, who for the joy that was set before him endured the cross, despising the shame, and is seated at the right hand of the throne of God."

What lessons can we learn from the Garden of Gethsemane? *First*, when we face a great test of our obedience, we must pray. God is there to hear, answer, test, and sustain us. Satan is there to distract, make us weary, tempt us to be disobedient and to choose our will instead of God's will.

Second, we learn to pray earnestly *before* we face a test of obedience. Jesus said to the disciples, "Watch and pray that you may not enter into temptation. The spirit indeed is willing, but the flesh is weak" (Mark 14:38). Few of us prepare ourselves through prayer for protection from temptation. In the Lord's Prayer, Jesus tells us to pray, "Lead us not into temptation, but deliver us from evil" (Matthew 6:13). Before you face what the world has to offer and before you do battle with Satan, make sure you have prayed for God's help and protection.

The battle is half-won if you want to avoid temptation enough to beg God to help you. When we pray, we are admitting our weakness. When we don't pray, it's usually because we don't take temptation seriously.

Third, some of our most earnest, agonizing prayers will go unanswered. Jesus's prayer did not change His circumstances or prevent His suffering. But it changed Him—His dependence, trust, obedience, and focus. I believe that God the Father had answered all of Jesus's prayers as He walked the dusty roads of Israel. Why didn't the Father answer the prayer of Gethsemane? Notice how it was phrased: Jesus didn't say, "Father get me out of here and receive me back into heaven." If He had prayed this, the Father would have answered. Rather, He prayed, "If it be possible…" That little word *if* showed His willingness to accept the Father's will. He didn't say, "Make it possible…" He prayed, "If it be possible…" That is a model for us to pray, "Lord, if it is Your will…" Some things we know are God's will, but there are dozens of circumstances where we don't know, and it is fine to pray, "If it be Your will, if it be possible…nevertheless, Your will be done."

Fourth, our cups of pain, injustice, hate, and abuse must be accepted as from the hand of God, not from the sinful, evil actions of men. Jesus did not speak about "the cup Satan has given Me, or the cup from the Sanhedrin, or the cup from Pilate, or the cup from the Roman soldiers." In submission, Jesus accepted the cup from His Father, "Shall I not drink the cup that the Father has given me?" (John 18:11). We can pray the same as we face the cup of cancer, chronic pain, disability, financial loss, natural disasters, accidents, divorce, and all kinds of abuse.

May we pray like Ivan, who was detained in a Russian concentration camp, enduring the horrors that took place in the Soviet Union. One day he closed his eyes and prayed. A fellow prisoner said to him, "Prayers won't get you out of here any faster." Ivan replied, "I do not pray to get out of prison, but to do the will of God." [37]

We are to bring our requests to the Father and be content to abide by His decision. We can pray earnestly for the sick; we can pray for a change of vocations; we can pray that we be kept from accident and harm. But we must always end with "nevertheless, not my will but Yours be done."

Most of us don't have nearly as much time to pray as Jesus did. But don't let that discourage you, because all of us can be in an attitude of prayerful dependence on God at all times. I've had the experience, as I'm sure you have, of being in a predicament or crisis, and immediately in my mind acknowledging my need for God's help, wisdom, or guidance. It's not necessarily how long we pray, important though that may be, but *what* we pray in that moment of need. Like Peter, who prayed only three words as he was going under the water, so we sometimes pray in desperation, "Lord, save me!" That's all that Jesus needed to hear.

Finally, life is not about us but about God and His will. Life is not about our happiness; life is about God's glory, even if it involves a cross. Will we obey even if it means suffering? Can you pray, "Your will be done on earth as it is in heaven?"

Taking God's Word to Heart

1. There will be times when our praying becomes a time of suffering. Meditate on Jesus's prayer and agony in the Garden of Gethsemane.

2. Think back over an agonizing decision you had to make. Did you surrender your will to God and accept His will? How did your decision turn out?

3. Read back over the four lessons we learn from Christ's experience in Gethsemane. How will this truth influence your life? Ask God to give you a heart that is willing to accept His will.

PRAYING FOR OUR CHILDREN

Mark 10:13-16—*And they were bringing children to him that he might touch them... "Let the children come to me; do not hinder them, for to such belongs the kingdom of God. Truly, I say to you, whoever does not receive the kingdom of God like a child shall not enter it." And he took them in his arms and blessed them, laying his hands on them.*

Matthew 15:28—*"O woman, great is your faith! Be it done for you as you desire." And her daughter was healed instantly.*

There is a story in the New Testament of a persistent mother, a Canaanite woman, who was desperate to get help for her tormented child. Jesus had just fed five thousand people on the shores of the Sea of Galilee. He then abruptly left that area to travel to the region of Tyre and Sidon (Matthew 15:21-28), a journey of several days over rugged terrain. It was unusual for Jesus and His disciples to enter territory where there was racial and religious strife, but Jesus was on a mission to reach a woman and her child, who was in great need.

We can only wonder how this woman knew that Jesus was in her town. As she approached Jesus and His disciples, she began crying out, "Have mercy on me, O Lord, Son of David; my daughter is severely oppressed by a demon" (15:22). This woman's attempt to find help for her distraught child was not an easy task due to the barriers of race, religion, and social standing she had to overcome to reach Jesus. She pleaded fearlessly for help, but Jesus and His disciples seemed not to notice her because "he did not answer her a word" (15:23). Jesus could have healed her child immediately, but He wanted to draw out the courage and faith that lay deep within this mother's heart. In fact, her faith was more important to Him than the healing that was about to take place. [38] When Jesus is silent, what should we do?

> This woman tells us that we must continue worshipping, asking, and believing. Even in our pain, confusion, doubt, and fear, we can come to Him with a humble attitude. God is listening. He is testing us, to see what is in our hearts. He wants us to verbalize our need, and to be willing to do whatever He asks of us, before He meets our need. We should never think that the silence of God means that He is indifferent to our need. [39]

The disciples became irritated: "Send her away, for she is crying out after us" (15:23). But Jesus broke His silence by saying, "I was sent only to the lost sheep of Israel" (15:24). He was referring to the fact that He had come first to the Jewish people to present Himself as their Messiah. Not to be put off or disappointed, she humbled herself and knelt before Him as she cried, "Lord, help me!" (15:25). She now called Him Lord, a further indication that she really believed that Jesus could heal her daughter.

Jesus replied with a new challenge: "It is not right to take the children's bread and throw it to the dogs" (15:26). He is implying that the Jews are God's children, and that the Gentiles are dogs. Harsh as this sounds, Jesus didn't use the common word for dogs, which referred to wild dogs that were mangy scavengers. Rather, He used the word for puppies, a household pet.

But still she did not take offense and walk away. She hung in there and boldly pressed on: "Yes, Lord...but even the dogs eat the crumbs that fall from their master's table" (15:27). It's just amazing how bold this mother was; she didn't flinch. She'd be happy just to get a few crumbs that no one else wanted.

At last, Jesus could no longer hold back His power and proclaimed,

"'O woman, great is your faith! Be it done for you as you desire.' And her daughter was healed instantly" (15:28).

Do you or I have the desire and stamina to persist long enough to receive for our child what they so desperately need? This is a great lesson in perseverance. We must continue to come to Jesus to get the help and answers for the problems that only He can change. We must believe that He has the power to change a hardened heart, heal a broken relationship, restore lost purity, deliver from addictions, and bring hope to a hopeless situation. [40]

How shall we pray for our children? Is there a formula or pattern we can follow?

As King David neared the end of his life and his reign over Israel, he gathered all the leaders and officials together so that he might give a charge to his son Solomon in their presence.

> "And you, Solomon my son, know the God of your father and serve him with a whole heart and with a willing mind, for the Lord searches all hearts and understands every plan and thought. If you seek him, he will be found by you, but if you forsake him, he will cast you off forever. Be careful now, for the Lord has chosen you to build a house for the sanctuary; be strong and do it...
>
> "Be strong and courageous and do it. Do not be afraid and do not be dismayed, for the Lord God, even my God, is with you. He will not leave you or forsake you, until all the work for the service of the house of the Lord is finished" (1 Chronicles 28:9-10,20).

These are wonderful words from a father who had blown it and knew the humiliation and consequences of his sin. Out of all of David's sons, God chose Solomon to sit on the throne of the kingdom of the Lord over Israel (28:5). This exhortation is an excellent example of what we can pray for our children and grandchildren.

We all want our children to grow up to be educated, successful people who are able to work hard and make enough money to live well and take care of themselves and their families, help those in need, and love and serve God. But are we more concerned about their secular success than their spiritual success? We act like it when we give them everything they want, satisfy all their cravings, let them read and watch whatever they want, and fail to give them spiritual instruction, thinking that the church will teach them what they should know about God.

Let us covenant to pray mightily that our children will desire to pursue and know God, to serve Him with a whole heart and a willing mind, that they be kept from evil and immorality, and strive to be godly people with integrity and moral character.

Before we can pray for our children or grandchildren, there are some necessary steps we must take. *First*, admit where we have failed them and the mistakes we have made in our relationship. *Second*, keep in mind that there is a great distinction between what we can do and what God can do. We cannot convert our children; that is God's work. But we can create a gospel-centered environment in which God can work. *Third*, represent the character of Christ to them. Practice what we preach. Be authentic and live the life before them that we are asking them to live.

Then we must pray that God in His merciful grace will accomplish the following in their lives for His glory:

1. That they become wise to salvation and know the Holy Scripture (2 Timothy 3:15)

2. That they grow in the grace and knowledge of the Lord (2 Peter 3:18)

3. That they trust in the Lord with all their heart and acknowledge Him (Proverbs 3:4,6)

4. That they endure hardship as a good soldier of Jesus Christ (2 Timothy 2:3-4)

5. That they fear the Lord and seek wisdom (Psalm 111:10)

6. That they walk in the counsel of the godly (Psalm 1:1)

7. That they delight in the law of the Lord (Psalm 1:2)

8. That when Christ calls them, no one would hinder them (Matthew 19:13-15) [41]

9. That they not be unequally yoked in intimate relationships (2 Corinthians 6:14) [42]

10. That they be kept from evil and be repentant when they sin (Matthew 6:13)

11. That they choose good friends (Proverbs 1:8-19)

12. That they be sexually pure (1 Corinthians 6:13-19; 1 Thessalonians 4:3-8)

13. That they have a heart to witness for Christ (Matthew 5:11-12)

14. That they love God more than they love sin (Matthew 22:37-39)

15. That they be willing to "throw their lives away for Christ" (Philippians 1:19-21)

The bottom line is that God has given us the responsibility to protect our children through faith and Scripture-based prayer. If we don't teach our children to follow Christ, the world will teach them not to. We will be held accountable if we fail to do our part in helping them escape the corruption of the world.

> One generation shall commend your works to another,
> and shall declare your mighty acts.
> (Psalm 145:4)

Taking God's Word to Heart

1. The Canaanite woman persistently overcame every obstacle to reach the heart of Jesus and convince Him to heal her

daughter. What are some obstacles that you must overcome to do the same for your child?

2. What character qualities of your child encourage you to seek divine help? What is your child's most urgent need that only God can provide?

3. Choose specific Scripture verses to pray for your child. Come up with a plan that will enable you to pray deeply and consistently for each of your children in specific ways and for specific things.

PRODIGALS

Jeremiah 31:16-17—*Thus says the LORD: "Keep your voice from weeping, and your eyes from tears, for there is a reward for your work, declares the LORD, and they shall come back from the land of the enemy. There is hope for your future, declares the LORD, and your children shall come back to their own country."*

Luke 15:17-18—*"But when he came to himself he said, 'How many of my father's hired servants have more than enough bread, but I perish here with hunger! I will arise and go to my father...'"*

My husband, Erwin, who is the senior pastor at the Moody Church in Chicago, started a series of prayer meetings that he dubbed POPS (Parents of Prodigals) and invited all who had wayward children to come together to pray for them. We knew of many parents with prodigals, but we were surprised at how quickly attendance at the prayer meeting doubled, and then tripled.

Many moms and dads are living with the pain of children who have strayed from what they have been taught and are now living rebellious, and often, destructive lives. Oh, the heartache and the tears that have been shed and the prayers that have been prayed for prodigal kids. History is filled with stories of mothers who have prayed for years for their wanderer, never giving up hope.

Children rebel for many obvious reasons—abuse, neglect, alcoholic and shame-based homes, poverty, wealth, a fatherless or motherless home, a traumatic family event, death of a parent, harsh and unloving parents—but sometimes there is no apparent explanation.

When we study the great men and women of the Bible, we are surprised to discover that there is often not a consistent pattern between the lifestyle of the parents and the lifestyle of their children. Evil parents sometimes have righteous children, and godly parents sometimes have evil children.

Ahaz was a wicked king, yet he had a son, Hezekiah, who "did what was right in the eyes of the Lord" (2 Kings 18:3). Then Hezekiah had a son named Manasseh who committed "abominations and has done things more evil than all that the Amorites did, who were before him" (2 Kings 21:11). It seems that the kings most devoted to God produced sons who became kings of idol worship, murder, and gross immorality.

The prophet Samuel was a righteous man who faithfully served God his entire life. We are surprised to learn that "his sons did not walk in his ways but turned aside after gain. They took bribes and perverted justice" (1 Samuel 8:3). It appears that the best of parenting does not guarantee righteous offspring. As one contemporary writer has said,

> The problem is that we all know incredible people who have come out of the most perverse, horrific family backgrounds who love the Lord Jesus with every fiber of their being AND are a delight to be around. But we also know people who were bibled, catechized, churched, separated, shrink-wrapped in modest gingham, who have been kept caffeine-, gluten-, and sugar-free since before the foundation of the world, who nonetheless turned out to be mean-spirited, arrogant monsters. [43]

A closer examination of this trend may give us valuable insight as to why a child rebels. Some Christian parents drive their children away from God by demanding that they follow a legalistic list of rules, which they hope will guarantee that their children become God-fearing and obedient. Once children figure out that they cannot live up to their parents' expectations, they just give up, rejecting the good with the bad. When a child does not turn out as the parents had hoped and prayed, parents may continually remind the child of their sin and failure to live up to what they have been taught.

Rules without relationship and rules without grace equal a rebellious child. Might this be the reason that Hezekiah's and Samuel's sons rebelled and turned away from the God of their fathers? When a child is accepted only for how consistently they obey the rules and for what they achieve, they will feel depressed and defeated. They will try to escape the tedious standards of their parents into a freedom that will allow them to do whatever they wish and not be condemned. We must keep in mind that it is in the nature of every child to disobey and to fight against our rules and God's rules. This shouldn't be a surprise as we look into our own sinful hearts.

What we as parents need is a better understanding of the gospel, which is God extending grace and forgiveness to us. We are all prodigals. None of us lives up to what we know and have been taught. None of us has kept the Ten Commandments perfectly. Rules show us that we are sinners, falling short of God's demand of perfection. Do we say that we are saved by the amazing gift of God's grace, but continue to live under the bondage of a list of demands? Jesus came to earth to live a perfect life, and then died for our imperfectness. He offers forgiveness, grace, love, and acceptance to us *while* we are rebelling and breaking His rules.

That's what happened to the prodigal in the parable Jesus told (Luke 15:11-32). The father was watching and waiting for his son to return so that he could show grace, mercy, love, forgiveness, and honor to him. He did not go looking for his son, condemning him for the disgrace he was bringing to the family. He waited for the son to return in repentance and humility. It is so important that we pray that the Holy Spirit will bring our children, young and old, to conviction and repentance.

There comes a time when parents must simply entrust to God children who have reached young adulthood rather than trying to convince and shame those children into repentance and submission to God. In fact, it is unwise to shame a child for any reason. Shame has its own lasting hurt and baggage. We must always extend grace—which is undeserved kindness—to our children. We should be mirrors of what God has done for us and affirm His goodness, grace, and kindness.

Dear one, have you personally experienced God's marvelous grace and forgiveness? If not, please open your heart to God's love and ask Him to forgive your sin and accept you as His daughter. He is watching and waiting for you to come home to Him.

Before we rebuke and discipline our children, we must make sure that we have established these seven parenting essentials:

- We have a relationship with our children in which they feel loved and accepted no matter what they do.

- We establish character-building, God-honoring, reasonable rules in our home.

- Our children know the rules, and we expect them to obey. Delayed obedience is disobedience. Don't give in to whining and begging. Be consistent.

- They know what the punishment will be if they disobey.

- We acknowledge that we have not always perfectly obeyed God, and He has had to discipline us.

- Our discipline matches our child's offense and is carried out in love and without anger.

- We quickly show grace to a repentant child, and extend forgiveness and love to restore the relationship. Since foolishness, selfishness, and self-protection are deeply imbedded in the heart of a child, grace should be applied generously as we bring up that child in the training and instruction of the Lord (Ephesians 6:4).

Why does the same home sometimes produce a prodigal *and* a

saint? Some children leave their upbringing because they have often been compared to a sibling and cannot live up to the goodness or accomplishments of a brother or sister. If a child grows up feeling unworthy, inferior, and rejected, they may rebel to punish their parents. Or they may work themselves to death to prove they are as worthy and accomplished as their sibling.

Another reason has to do with how we respond to our children when they express doubts and question our Christianity. Some just fall in line, never questioning our beliefs and rules. But some children are born with doubts, demanding an explanation for everything. They push us to the limits of our theology and sanity. But how we respond is crucial—it can make or break that child. If we think that a questioning child is a rebellious child, and we respond in condemnation and ridicule and impose greater restrictions upon them, it may cause them to truly rebel and reject us and our God.

On the other hand, by treating a questioning and doubt-filled child with respect, grace, and love, by listening to them express themselves, and by guiding them to investigate and compare our beliefs with others, they will do so with an open mind, and they will respect and want to please us. [44]

Many a prodigal has said, "I hate my parents, and I hate their God." How many parents need to repent before their prodigal does? Countless numbers. Wise parents will repent of their own failures, harshness, misunderstanding, severe discipline, comparison, suspicion, and lack of love and compassion. Many a child who has turned from the faith has been reconciled when the parents humbled themselves and apologized for their mistakes and failures. We must always keep the door open for a wayward child.

Wise parents will love their prodigals without continuing to remind them of how wrong they are in their rebellion. We must all learn from our mistakes and bad decisions. We must all come to our senses while in the far country, just as the prodigal of old did. Hunger and the smell of pigs finally made him "come to his senses" (Luke 15:17 NIV). For some, it will be jail time; for others it might be a failed marriage, the betrayal of friends, homelessness, financial ruin, a painful disease, or a devastating accident.

Are you heartbroken over a son or daughter who is running from God?

> One of the most powerful means of grace in children's lives is the gift of praying parents. And though untold weeks and years can elapse without getting the answer they hope for, this often toilsome process is part of what He uses to sanctify believing parents, draw them closer to Him, and amaze them with the lengths He is willing to travel to rescue their children. Don't stop praying. Keep laying hold of God. The last chapter is not yet written. He is still weaving your faithful, earnest prayers into His story for their lives. [45]

"Just so, I tell you, there will be more joy in heaven over one sinner who repents than over ninety-nine righteous persons who need no repentance" (Luke 15:7).

Taking God's Word to Heart

1. Why do parents often struggle with false guilt when they have a prodigal child? When might their guilt be justified?

2. Evaluate the ways and means by which a child becomes a prodigal. If you have a prodigal in your home, what might you be contributing toward that process in your relationship with that child?

3. List all the lessons you can think of that the father of the prodigal in Luke 15:11-32 has to teach us about how to respond to a wayward child. Pray earnestly for your prodigal child. Ask God to enable you to be the means by which they will return to God and to you.

PROTECTING OUR CHILDREN

Deuteronomy 6:6-7— *"And these words that I command you today shall be on your heart. You shall teach them diligently to your children, and shall talk of them when you sit in your house, and when you walk by the way, and when you lie down and when you arise."*

Proverbs 6:20-22—
My son [daughter] keep your father's commandment, and forsake not your mother's teaching.
Bind them on your heart always; tie them around your neck.
When you walk, they will lead you; when you lie down, they will watch over you; and when you awake, they will talk with you.

2 Corinthians 6:17-18— *"Therefore go out from their midst, and be separate from them, says the Lord, and touch no unclean thing; then I will welcome you, and I will be a father to you, and you shall be sons and daughters to me, says the Lord Almighty."*

As parents we face tremendous challenges because our children face grave dangers. We have two responsibilities in protecting our children: one is to keep them as far as possible from evil influences, and the second is to pray for God's guidance and protection so that they will follow His plan for their lives. Both of these challenges must be met with determination, discernment, and consistency.

A monster has invaded our homes, passing through the bricks, walls, doors, and windows, and is stealing the hearts and souls of our children, leaving their bodies intact. It is the monster of technology and the entertainment industry.

Evil people work day and night to come up with ways to capture your child, steal their innocence, and destroy their dreams. The Internet and cell phones provide easy access to pornography, social websites with predators, video games with occultism and violence. Pornography is capturing the interest of younger and younger kids. It used to be that boys discovered it at puberty, but now they are exposed to it as young as seven and eight. It is the thief of innocence as it awakens their curiosity and desires.

Children are molested by coaches, teachers, priests, babysitters, stepfathers, and boyfriends of a mother or sister. Molested children enter a dark place in their souls to hide their shame. I know of a situation where unsuspecting parents entrusted their son's afterschool care to the principal of the Christian school he attended. This boy was molested by this man many times and was shamed and threatened into silence. It dramatically affected his life into adulthood, though his parents did not know about it until years later.

Most parents don't have a clue. Society provides so many opportunities for children to be left unprotected and neglected. The challenges of life for single parents and stepparents, for blended families and dysfunctional families, often leave children unsupervised in their homes. The schools provide sex education that promotes pleasure without responsibility or guilt. Libraries do not protect children from exposure to pornography on their computers. Your kids will see and hear things from their friends, in other homes, and in school that you object to but are unaware of. And all of this has the power to influence them and turn their hearts away from God.

Your home may be truly safe, but not all of your kids' friends' homes are. Not even the Christian families you think you know. There is a wide range of morals and standards even among Christians.

The lack of discernment of many parents is appalling. They act as though they don't know what's going on in society. It is willing ignorance. Many parents are too lax and naïve about what their children watch on TV. They think it is all right for their kids to look at scantily clad women in dancing competitions, see young people and adults in sexual situations, and listen to immoral innuendos and obscenities.

Where has the authority of the parents gone? They give into whining, begging, and tantrums. Sure, parents are exhausted from their jobs and other responsibilities, but failing to protect their children through the lack of discernment and weariness is a serious matter. God will hold parents accountable. So *be the parent!*

What can we do to protect our children and families?

1. Get your act together.

Parents lose moral authority because they are yielding to some of the same temptations they are trying to steer their children away from. Sometimes we must do drastic things. If we can't control our use of the television, computer, and video games, perhaps we should get rid of them.

Live pure lives before your children. Model the behavior you want from them. Don't watch something you don't want your children to watch.

> Turn my eyes from looking at worthless things;
> and give me life in your ways.
>
> (Psalm 119:37)

You can't fight these battles on your own. The forces are too powerful and strong. You must connect with others through Bible studies, accountability partners, men's and women's support groups, and prayer meetings.

2. Be unified and consistent.

Kids will exploit a lack of agreement between their mother and father. Be unified in your strategy and develop a plan for your home. Make a list of rules and go over it with your children. Explain and discuss why you have chosen these particular things so that your home will run smoothly and that everyone will be safe. Right up front, let them know what discipline will take place if they break the rules. Discipline appropriately and consistently.

Develop a good relationship with each child from an early age. Rules without relationship equal rebellion. If you are too strict or self-righteous and preach sermons to them, their hearts and minds will turn away from you. So develop relationship first, then strategy.

3. Teach your children how to abstain from the passions of the flesh.

Femininity and masculinity should be modeled. As your kids get older, talk with them about the desires of their bodies and minds, and why and how they can control them rather than being controlled by them. Share in a general way about your own struggles and failures when you were growing up. Listen to your kids, ask questions, and then talk without shaming or condemning them. Shame fuels addiction.

Talk about the process that took place as Adam and Eve listened to the lies of the serpent and chose to disobey God. Talk about Joseph and his choices to obey God rather than the passions of his flesh. Role-play some scenarios with your daughter about what she should do in certain situations or what to do when a boy tries to take advantage of her. Teach her what modesty is and why it is important. Teach your son the proper words and behavior that will show respect to girls.

Talk about God's grace and redeeming power, forgiveness, and restoration. Teach them that failure is not the end of hope and life. That's Satan's lie, which can lead to suicide in teenagers who think they have messed up too bad to go on. God is always waiting to lift us up when we fall.

4. Do not allow any unfiltered computers, websites, or mobile devices in your home.

Mobile devices should be used under strict supervision. No child needs an iPhone. Place your home computer in the family room, situated so that it is clearly visible to everyone. Under no circumstances should a child have a computer or TV in their bedroom. Your children do not have unrestricted rights to privacy in their bedrooms. Kids should understand that you can come in and check their room regularly.

You might be thinking, *But I trust my child.* Moms, this is naïve. The passions of the flesh are warring against him or her. If your child says to you, "You don't trust me," you can tell them, "You're right, I don't. Neither do I trust myself. In order for all of us to be safe, this is what we're going to do."

5. Know what's being taught in your children's schools and in friends' homes.

Kevin Jennings, founder of the Gay, Lesbian, and Straight Education Network (GLSEN), called for the "queering" of elementary education. He told children "to explore their sexual identities and urged K-5 teachers to incorporate homosexual behavior themes in their classrooms!" [46]

Also be cautious about allowing your child to visit in the homes of their friends. Kids have been introduced to pornography and drugs and have been sexually abused in the home of someone their parents trusted. I know of one little girl who was molested by her friend's older brother when she went over to the friend's home to play.

6. Do not shame your children.

If a child is found viewing an inappropriate site, do not shame them. Ask if they have done this before and what got them interested. Tell them why it is wrong and destructive. Teach them that both the forgiveness and cleansing of God is essential to clear their conscience. Pray with them, and make sure that they know you love them and they can talk to you anytime they need help with this. Tell them you will be checking on them and monitoring their computer use.

7. Develop family camaraderie.

Take responsibility for one another. Eat dinner together whenever possible. Instead of playing video games or watching television, play table games, read books, put puzzles together, or just talk. Get to know your kids' friends by inviting them into your home. As you observe them, you can then talk with your child about their friends and warn them about any concerns you may have.

Show respect and honor to your children. No yelling, slapping, anger, inconsistent discipline, or belittling. Anger fuels rebellion and addictions. "Fathers do not provoke [exasperate] your children to anger, but bring them up in the discipline and instruction of the Lord" (Ephesians 6:4).

8. Lead your child to saving faith in Christ.

Make sure your child understands the gospel. Explain that everyone has disobeyed God in many ways and we are all sinners. God loved people so much that He sent His Son Jesus to the earth to die for their sins, and when we accept Jesus's death on the cross we'll be forgiven and have eternal life. The Holy Spirit (explain who He is) comes to live within us and help us obey God and our parents.

Some of you may be wondering, "How do I reclaim the mind and heart of my child?" It is never too late to begin at the beginning. Humble yourself and ask forgiveness for your mistakes and failures as a parent. Tell your child you have not been obedient to God's instructions to guide and protect them. Admit that you have failed in allowing them to do certain things and go certain places. It's a new day—it's time to make some changes in your family activities and rules. Tell them that before God you are taking your parental responsibility to guide them back to life, hope, peace, and love. Don't blame your child for where he or she is. In their immaturity, rebellion and your lack of protection, they have been led astray and deceived.

Keep committing your child to God. Love them unconditionally. Don't alienate them any further by judgmental comments. Pray earnestly for your child. Read, study, and memorize the Word. If needed, enlist the help of your pastor or a counselor. There are many books, websites, and online resources to turn to.

We must personally develop a passion for God that is greater than our passions of the flesh. It is only then that we can escape the corruption of the world and show our children how to live victoriously and successfully.

Taking God's Word to Heart

1. Think through the various technologies by which the enemy enters our homes today. How can we protect our children from the constant assault upon their hearts and minds?

2. Are you aware of all the daily influences on your children— what they are being taught in school, who their friends are, the atmosphere of their friends' homes, what movies and shows they are watching, what they are looking at on their computers and phones? Do you have the proper filters in place?

3. What compromises are you making that are affecting your children? What changes do you need to make?

SEXUAL HEALING

Psalm 51:7,9-10,12—
Purge me with hyssop, and I shall be clean;
wash me, and I shall be whiter than snow...
Hide your face from my sins,
and blot out all my iniquities.
Create in me a clean heart, O God,
and renew a right spirit within me...
Restore to me the joy of your salvation,
and uphold me with a willing spirit.

Luke 7:47,50— *"Therefore I tell you, her sins, which*
are many, are forgiven—for she loved much. But he
who is forgiven little, loves little."...And he said to the
woman, "Your faith has saved you; go in peace."

John 10:10— *"The thief comes only to steal*
and kill and destroy. I came that they may
have life and have it abundantly."

Sexual brokenness is the guilt and shame that come from impure sexual relationships, which have plagued the human race since the beginning. From kings to commoners, the Bible contains many accounts of immorality and warns of the sin and sorrow that result from them. Long before enticements of the printed page and modern technology increased temptation and inflamed passions, people have participated in all kinds of illicit relationships, either consensual or coerced.

It is important for us to understand the nature of sexual bonding that forms when two individuals are connected in some way sexually— by mutual agreement, verbal manipulation, rape, abuse, molestation, or inappropriate touching. First Corinthians 6:16 boldly asks, "Do you not know that he who is joined to a prostitute becomes one body with her? For, as it is written, 'The two will become one flesh.'" This verse teaches us that even in lustful sexual relationships where there is no pretense of love, the participants are joined together so that they are "one flesh." A spiritual union has been formed that is not based on trust and the permanent covenant of marriage. It is a "soul tie" that is difficult to break emotionally and psychologically.

This is especially true for women. After a sexual union, a woman's spirit latches on to a man and wants to love, bless, fulfill, and refresh his heart and soul. Her spirit doesn't forget the union and she seeks for that man. But when the relationship ends and the man moves on, part of her spirit goes with him. He took her love and used her for his pleasure, leaving her soul feeling wasted. Eventually, she will hate that man and hate herself for giving her body, soul, and spirit to a man who didn't love her.

It is possible to be aware of someone's desire for us, which can be a powerful magnet to them. Because God created women with the need to be noticed, admired, and touched, we must be very careful to maintain an emotional and physical distance from such a person. This is also a word of caution to those who are in ministry and counseling, bearing the burden of others. We must be careful to not identify or empathize with someone else's sin or shame to the point that we are drawn to them and become defiled. We must be sober-minded and alert because our adversary the devil is prowling around like a roaring lion, looking for someone to devour. We must resist the evil one, remaining firm in our faith (1 Peter 5:8-9). Satan wants to destroy our souls, and he will try to get us to be immoral to accomplish that.

These kinds of relationships result in feelings of guilt, shame, insecurity, and betrayal, which go on to produce anger, self-hatred, mistrust, and sexual confusion. Sadly, this in turn may open the door to a life of promiscuity and difficulty in forming a lasting bond of commitment in marriage. As one woman said, "After I had sex with my boyfriend, I heard a voice inside my head that said, 'Now that you are defiled, you might as well find other lovers.'" The path back to wholeness through forgiveness, healing, and restoration is often long and painful, but God is waiting to help us begin a new life of hope and peace far away from our past.

Some people who are sexually broken must take personal responsibility for deliberately crossing moral boundaries they knew to be sinful. Others had harmful sexual experiences forced upon them; they were not at fault and bear no responsibility for their brokenness. About one in four girls are molested, usually within the family structure. This evil may be perpetrated by a father, brother, uncle, grandfather, friend of the family, babysitter, childhood friend, neighbor, or a trusted person in authority. Boys, too, are molested by some of the same kinds of individuals.

What happens to the one who has been misused and violated? They have been betrayed, defiled, shamed, and their innocence and purity stolen. They are made to feel worthless and often become confused about their sexual identity. Their bodies may become just a shell covering an empty soul. Abused and abandoned by those they trusted, they are sometimes led down paths to further sexual abuse or into promiscuity.

How does an abused person recover from their pain and wounds, have their soul restored, and reclaim their purity? *First*, healing begins with the crucial choice of forgiving the abuser. Often, counseling with a trusted and qualified person is necessary to reach the place of confidence and courage needed in order to forgive. *Second*, they need to understand who they are in Jesus Christ—loved, accepted, forgiven. The river of living water can wash them and make them as white as snow in His shed blood. *Third*, it is very important to study the Bible and spend much time in prayer. *Fourth*, support and acceptance from understanding, compassionate believers will give encouragement and hasten the healing process. (The chapter "Woundedness and Healing" gives more in-depth help on healing from the past.)

Those who have chosen to cross moral boundaries are often quick to rationalize their behavior even though a quiet voice troubles their conscience and distracts them. What they thought was a refreshing oasis turned out to be a poisoned well. Someone has said, "Sexual liaisons promise like a god but pay like the devil." How does someone who has been immoral, whether once or many times with multiple partners, recover? How do they heal from guilt, a sense of defilement, and sorrow over their sin?

First, there must be genuine repentance all the way through to the deepest core of our being. There should be profound sorrow over our sin, confession, and accepting God's forgiveness, because He forgives all our iniquity and removes our transgressions as far as the east is from the west (Psalm 103:3,12). God always honors the truth of this verse, "If we confess our sins, he is faithful and just to forgive us our sins and to cleanse us from all unrighteousness" (1 John 1:9). We need to ask God to wash our spirit, mind, and body in the blood of Jesus and to restore our purity.

Second, we must remove ourselves from the sinful relationship. This may be difficult if it involves moving or changing jobs, or if the other person is unstable and dangerous. We must pray earnestly for wisdom and seek the help of family, friends, and authorities of the law and court, if needed.

Third, we must give our needs to God. If we struggle with the desire to flirt and tempt men to lust for us, we must bring that to the cross and put it to death. We must choose to live a righteous life and put to death any want or habit that will lead us back into immorality.

Fourth, we must begin to fill our life and heart with Scripture and prayer. We need to eliminate sensual reading material and media temptations. We need to become part of a community of believers in a church that teaches the truth of God's Word, join a Bible study, and choose a maturing believer to be an accountability partner.

I believe it is necessary to pray very specific prayers to break sexual bonding and reclaim what Satan has stolen from us. Here is a suggested prayer you may find helpful:

> By the authority of the Lord Jesus Christ, who has forgiven my sins and washed me clean in His blood, I loose my spirit from every man or woman I have had a sexual relationship with. I break the sexual bond that was made with _____. I direct my spirit to forget that union. In the name of Jesus, I break the power of that inner vow that is locking me up and loose myself to freedom in Christ.
>
> Almighty heavenly Father, gird me with truth and protect the sanctity of my sexuality. Teach me the holiness of sexual union. Restore my purity and keep my body and sexual love only for my future husband. I choose to wait for him. (If you are already married: I choose to be faithful to my husband. Let me enjoy the beauty and glory of marital sex with him only.) Flood my body, soul, and spirit with Your amazing grace, until I feel clean and pure again. With all my heart, soul, spirit, mind, and body, I thank You and love You, Lord. In Jesus's name, amen.

If you continue to feel guilty or harassed by Satan, you can speak these words or something similar:

> What God has pronounced clean, you may not call unclean. I am chosen, precious, valuable, forgiven, and made new by the blood of Christ. I have been restored to purity, and you have no authority to condemn me for past sins. I reject all guilt you bring to me and forbid you to harass me. "Who shall bring any charge against God's elect. It is God who justifies. Who is to condemn? Christ Jesus is the one who died—more than that, who was raised—who is at the right hand of God, who indeed is interceding for [me]" (Romans 8:33-34). Be gone, Satan! I have nothing more to say to you.

Even though our memories will never entirely let us forget what we have done or what was done against us, the power of our past can be broken. God will take and use it for His glory and make it work together for good in our lives, bringing hope and healing to others.

Taking God's Word to Heart

1. What is sexual bonding and how does it affect our lives?

2. How does an abused person recover from their pain and wounds, have their soul restored, and reclaim their purity?

3. Explain the steps someone who has been immoral must take to recover from guilt, break the sexual bond, and heal from the sorrow over their sin.

SHAME [47]

Psalm 25:2-3—*O my God, in you I trust;*
let me not be put to shame;
let not my enemies exult over me.
Indeed, none who wait for you shall be put to shame.

Romans 8:1—*There is therefore now no*
condemnation for those who are in Christ Jesus.

We all know the painful, powerful feeling of shame. It is a deep-seated sadness of the soul that we have disappointed ourselves, others, and most of all, God. Shame can be defined as a sense of disgrace, humiliation, or embarrassment that develops from things we have done or because of what others have done to us. Shame tells us that not just our behavior is wrong but that we are significantly damaged. Our sense of personal honor and integrity has been bargained away.

There are two kinds of shame. *Objective shame* comes from violating God's standard by our own sin. This is healthy shame that leads us to seek God's forgiveness. *Subjective shame* is forced upon us by the sin of others against us. This is an unhealthy shame that condemns us for what others have done and for which they must seek God's forgiveness.

Shame was not a part of the original creation, for we read, "The man and his wife were both naked, and were not ashamed" (Genesis 2:25). In this account nakedness is not just a physical condition, it represents being in right relationship with God. They were perfect and in perfect fellowship with their Creator; therefore, there was nothing to be ashamed of.

Sin in all forms produces shame. Before Adam and Eve disobeyed God, they were not ashamed of their nakedness or any of their actions. After they sinned, they were ashamed because their moral consciousness had been awakened, just as the serpent had promised, "For God knows that when you eat of it your eyes will be opened, and you will be like God, knowing good and evil" (Genesis 3:5). They would personally experience the effects of evil in their lives, as would their children and, subsequently, the entire human race. God was now a rival who must be defied. Unknown to them, there would be no way back to Eden or innocence.

To hide their nakedness, Adam and Eve sewed fig leaves together to make a covering, and when they heard God walking in the garden, they hid. The ones who had felt no shame, now cowered in fear of being exposed to the holiness of the Almighty whom they had disobeyed.

But thankfully, the Creator did not abandon them. Though He knew exactly where they were hiding, His search for them was the beginning of grace. He called out to the distraught man, forcing him to reveal himself and to admit their disobedience. God Himself made them garments of animal skin to cover their shame—this was the first act of grace for the human race. *Grace is the answer to shame.*

If objective shame is the result of a sin I need forgiveness for, subjective shame is imposed upon me by others, most likely members of the family. Children brought up in a home where there is alcoholism, addictions, and various kinds of abuse feel shame through no fault of their own. Some parents seek to control their children through unfair or false accusations and by excessive, anger-fueled discipline. This produces a feeling of powerlessness in a child, which results in anger and control issues in their adulthood.

Sexual abuse creates incredible shame. A woman who was abused as a child said that when she went to school she thought her classmates could see inside of her; it was as if they all knew her terrible secrets. She felt exposed and diminished, unable to look her teacher or friends in the eye.

A shame-based home is one where there is ridicule, neglect, criticism, negativism, comparison, blaming, humiliation, shouting, or accusing for any infraction, whether real or imagined. This creates a sense of emotional numbness, loneliness, and distrust.

The effects of unresolved shame in adulthood are enormous. *First*, these people may become paranoid and suspicious of others, always expecting betrayal and humiliation. They feel threatened and are constantly on guard to protect themselves from probing questions or suggestions of improvement.

Second, unresolved shame can lead to a life of crime. A child who has been controlled, abused, and neglected may grow up to lash out in anger against their parents, others, and God. Breaking the law becomes their way of getting revenge and finally exercising power in their powerless world.

Third, in a shame-based home where parental love and acceptance is based only on performance, a perfectionist is often created. They may become judgmental and critical with contempt for those who don't try as hard or do as well as they do. Of course, some jobs require perfection, such as that of a pilot or a surgeon. But there are other times when standards are so elevated and the need to blame so strong that perfectionism becomes harmful to relationships.

Fourth, people who feel shamed and flawed often see themselves as victims. They think they deserve to be abused and shamed, and they become a doormat for others. Many find it difficult to accept demonstrations of genuine love and compassion. They are desperate for someone to love them, but when an effort is made, they react as though they are unworthy of anyone's love.

It is no surprise that part of the suffering of hell is eternal shame: "Many of those who sleep in the dust of the earth shall awake, some to everlasting life, and some to shame and everlasting contempt" (Daniel 12:2). It is difficult to imagine what hell will be like, but being totally exposed in the sight of God and in the presence of others, without a grace-covering or a place to hide, without God's forgiveness…that would be hell.

God's prescription for healing from shame begins with a willingness to believe that we are worthy of God's grace. There is more grace in God's heart than there is sin in our past. The cure for feeling unworthy of God's attention and acceptance is to discover that we have already been accepted by the One who matters most, "To the praise of His glorious grace, with which he has blessed us in the Beloved" (Ephesians 1:6).

In an excellent article titled "Shame Crucified," Rodney Clapp discusses how Christ delivers us from shame. He says that the most dreadful thing about the cross was not the physical suffering but the shame. Jesus was subjected to personal humiliation and disgrace. "Christ redeemed us from the curse of the law by becoming a curse for us—for it is written, 'Cursed is everyone who is hanged on a tree'" (Galatians 3:13).

Let us ask a series of questions that Clapp would have us answer by looking to the experience of Jesus. [48]

- Does shame bind us? Jesus was bound.

- Does shame destroy our reputation? He is despised and rejected of men.

- Does shame reduce us to silence? He was led as a lamb to the slaughter and as a sheep before His shearers is silent, so He opened not His mouth.

- Does shame lead to abandonment? Jesus cried out, "My God, my God, why have you forsaken me?"

- Does shame diminish us? He was crucified naked, exposed for gawkers to see.

How did Jesus respond to this shame? With endurance, scorn, and contempt: "who for the joy set before him, endured the cross, scorning its shame, and sat down at the right hand of the throne of God"

(Hebrews 12:2 NIV). Jesus proved that shame does not need to permanently disable or destroy anyone. Because of Jesus's victory on the cross, shame has lost its power and sting. "He shamed, shame." [49]

As Clapp writes, "The Cross creates a community of people, who are no longer afraid of being defined and destroyed by shame, can admit their failures and allow their neediness." [50] No one has been so disgraced or defiled that they are unworthy of human compassion and love. God's love and grace are waiting for those who feel worthless, humiliated, and unloved. "But where sin increased, grace abounded all the more" (Romans 5:20).

Tamar, one of King David's daughters, was raped by her half-brother Amnon. Her anguished cry comes to us from across the ages, "And Tamar put ashes on her head and tore the long robe that she wore [a symbol of her virginity]. And she laid her hand on her head and went away, crying aloud as she went" (2 Samuel 13:19). The ashes were a sign of her humiliation and shame.

How does God restore people like this? Isaiah predicts that with the coming of Christ, the brokenhearted will receive healing, the prisoners will be released, and those who mourn will be comforted. And He will

> bestow on them a crown of beauty
>   instead of ashes,
> the oil of joy
>   instead of mourning,
> and a garment of praise
>   instead of a spirit of despair.
>   (Isaiah 61:3 NIV)

The elements of a funeral—ashes, mourning, despair—will give way to a celebration. These are beautiful word pictures. A crown of beauty—signifies honor; soothing oil—healing; a garment of praise—hope. Shame has lost its power over us, and we are free to be beautiful, joyful, and covered by God's righteousness. Elisabeth Elliot said, "Of one thing I am perfectly sure: God's story never ends with ashes."

Beloved one, you may still be wondering what steps you must take to be delivered from your shame. First, if you have never done so, ask Jesus to be your Savior, to forgive and cleanse you. Second, confess all of your sin that has caused you shame. Third, if your shame was caused by someone else's sin against you, by God's grace choose to forgive that person. Ask Jesus to release you from the power of that shameful sin and to cleanse you. Fourth, gather up all of your shame like trash scattered over a yard and hand it to your Savior. He has already scorned your shame on the cross. It's not your burden to carry any longer. Fifth, read the healing words of Psalm 25:1-3 as a prayer to God as often as you need to:

> To you, O LORD, I lift up my soul.
> O my God, in you I trust;
>   let me not be put to shame;
>   let not my enemies exult over me.
> Indeed, none who wait for you shall be put to shame.

Let us choose to leave our shame at the cross where Jesus left His.

Taking God's Word to Heart

1. If you have experienced shame, how has it made you feel, and how has it affected your life?

2. Write out your understanding of how Jesus Christ endured the shame of the cross. How does His victory enable us to overcome our shame?

3. What steps do you need to take to be freed from shame and begin to heal?

TEMPTATION

1 Corinthians 10:13—*No temptation has overtaken you that is not common to man. God is faithful, and he will not let you be tempted beyond your ability, but with the temptation he will also provide the way of escape, that you may be able to endure it.*

Matthew 4:10—*"Be gone, Satan! For it is written, 'You shall worship the Lord your God and him only shall you serve.'"*

Romans 13:14—*But put on the Lord Jesus Christ, and make no provision for the flesh, to gratify its desires.*

Temptations come to us anywhere, anytime, and in many ways. It is *not* a sin to be tempted. Jesus was tempted directly by Satan and He did not sin. Temptation is not evil, but the act of giving in to it is sinful. All of us know of dedicated Christian men and women who faced temptation and were defeated by it. The Bible records the stories of many people chosen by God who succumbed to temptation. Satan is our enemy. He wants us to fall into sin and disobedience.

Ever since the serpent tempted Eve to disobey God, he has been tempting the human race to do the same. Temptation comes from three sources: the desires of the flesh, the desires of the eyes, and the pride of life (1 John 2:16). Satan is always involved in temptation.

What does Satan the serpent want for us? Exactly what he wanted for Eve—separation from God. He lies and tricks us into thinking that sin looks good and feels good, that for a moment of pleasure, we might be like him, rebelling against God. Never mind the troubled conscience and sorrow that will follow later.

Let's take a close look at the classic battle between Christ and Satan in the Judean desert (Matthew 4:1-11). Jesus Christ had just been baptized by John the Baptist and heard the voice of His Father from heaven, "This is my beloved Son, with whom I am well pleased" (Matthew 3:17). On the heels of this great spiritually confirming experience, the devil attacks Him. Jesus turns from a glimpse into heaven to a glimpse into hell. "The temptations are a diabolical attempt to subvert God's plan for human redemption by causing Jesus to fall into sin and disobedience, thus disqualifying him as the sinless Savior." [51]

"Then Jesus was led up by the Spirit into the wilderness to be tempted by the devil" (Matthew 4:1). Does it seem strange that the Holy Spirit led Jesus to be tempted by the devil? From our standpoint, yes, but God the Father and God the Holy Spirit meant it to be a test. Before Jesus began His public ministry, He established authority over Satan, who questioned His authenticity that had just been established by John the Baptist and His Father in heaven—"if you are the Son of God" (4:3,6). The devil effectively turned this test into a temptation to try to separate Christ from His Father and bypass the cross. "So Satan, with unmitigated audacity, attempts to do what he most surely knew was impossible. *He tries to triumph over the very Christ who created him!*" [52]

The *first* temptation does not seem unreasonable—satisfy your hunger. It was one of physical gratification, a desire of the flesh: "If you are the Son of God, command these stones to become loaves of bread" (4:3). For Jesus to end His fast of forty days at Satan's directive would mean independence from His Father. It was not time for Christ to perform a miracle, which would interfere with the divine plan. Miracles would be part of His ministry later, but not now. Thus, the first temptation was for Jesus to turn away from His Father's will.

The *second* temptation is a risky request from Satan—satisfy your pride. It was one of personal achievement and glory—the pride of life: "If you are the Son of God, throw yourself down, for it is written, 'He will command his angels concerning you,' and 'On their hands they will bear you up, lest you strike your foot against a stone'" (4:6). For Jesus to jump from such a great height as the pinnacle of the temple unharmed would have been a spectacular display of His messianic claims.

Satan became bolder. Jesus had quoted Scripture to him as a rebuke in the first temptation. Arrogantly, the devil quotes from Psalm 91 in a deliberate misuse of Scripture to try to influence Jesus. "Satan quotes Scripture for evil motives. By using Scripture, he wanted to thwart Christ's ability to quote Scripture. He would wrest the Sword of the Spirit from Christ's hands and use it for his own sinister purposes."[53] Thus, the second temptation was for Jesus to turn away from the Word of God.

The *third* temptation was a shocking demand from Satan—satisfy Your authority with power. For Jesus to accept Satan's offer of great possessions and glory by worshipping him would have kept Jesus from dying on the cross to secure our redemption from sin and Satan. That's what Satan really wanted. "Again, the devil took him to a very high mountain and showed him all the kingdoms of the world and their glory. And he said to him, 'All these I will give you, if you will fall down and worship me'" (4:8-9). Would Christ exchange the love of His Father for the worship of Satan?

But Jesus called Satan's bluff: "Then Jesus said to him, 'Be gone, Satan! For it is written, "You shall worship the Lord your God and him only shall you serve"'" (4:10). Jesus Christ demonstrated who was Lord. He was obedient. He passed the test. Satan had gambled and lost, so the battle between the kingdoms of this world and the kingdom of Christ has continued to this day. Thus, the third temptation was for Jesus to turn away from the cross.

What lessons can we learn from Jesus on how to behave when we're tempted? Jesus wasn't just lucky when He managed to get rid of Satan without giving into temptation. He carried out every command in 1 Peter 5:6-9 (NIV):

> *Humble* yourselves, therefore, under God's mighty hand, that he may lift you up in due time. *Cast* all your anxiety on him because he cares for you.

> *Be alert and of sober mind.* Your enemy the devil prowls around like a roaring lion looking for someone to devour. *Resist him, standing firm in the faith,* because you know that the family of believers throughout the world is undergoing the same kind of sufferings.

The first temptation (turning stones into bread) is one that Jesus could have easily handled. But He *humbled himself, cast His anxieties* onto the Father, and waited to eat at the appointed time.

The second temptation (jumping from a great height and being caught by angels) is one that Jesus could have justified doing. But He maintained a *sober mind* and remained *alert,* quoting Scripture and standing against the wiles of the devil (Ephesians 6:11). It would have been presumptuous for Him to think He would be protected while disobeying His Father.

The third temptation (worship the devil) is one that Jesus could not do, for God cannot worship evil. Jesus *resisted the devil* and *stood firm in His faith,* quoting Scripture back to Satan and extinguishing the flaming darts of the evil one (Ephesians 6:16). He trusted that His Father knew best and would both deliver Him and provide for His needs at the right time. The old devil had to flee from Jesus (James 4:7). Satan knew when he had been whipped.

Beloved women, God will test our love and loyalty through painful circumstances, trials, difficult people, illness, and our own sinful desires. Remember that our adversary the devil is prowling around like a roaring lion, seeking someone to devour. He will turn our tests into temptations. When the passions of our heart and body are screaming to be satisfied, Satan will be waiting to fulfill them in sinful ways that will eventually bring sorrow and heartache. They will come to us in a hundred ways, seducing us to meet our needs, wants, and longings outside of God's will and appointed time. He will present many appealing, attractive, exciting, fulfilling—but sinful and deadly—options. I beg you not to give in to Satan's lies and deception.

Some time ago I was shopping at a popular store. As I stepped to the counter to pay, the woman ringing up my purchases said sadly, "I just don't know what I'm going to do." I glanced down where her cell phone lay next to the register and asked her what had happened.

"It's my husband," she said. "He's an alcoholic and causing me a lot of trouble. I knew I shouldn't have married him, but I wanted him, and I told God, 'I can handle this one.' But it hasn't gone very well, and now I feel desperate."

I reached my hand out to touch hers and said, "God loves you and will forgive you. He will help you, but you must talk to Him and confess your disobedience. Then ask God to give you grace and wisdom to know what to do."

Her eyes filled with tears as she thanked me, and we both leaned over the counter toward each other for a hug. I asked her name and told her that I would be praying for her. As I turned to leave, *my* eyes filled with tears. Her burden and regret seemed to hang around her shoulders like a heavy coat. For the next few days, I prayed for this woman several times, entrusting her into God's care for wisdom, mercy, and grace.

God wants you and me to obey His will and His Word, and to stay near the cross for protection and safety. We must humble ourselves before God. Give our anxieties to Him. Be sober-minded. Be alert. Resist the devil. Quote appropriate Scripture. Stand firm in our faith. Pray for deliverance from evil (Matthew 6:13). Put on the armor of God to stand against the devil's schemes (Ephesians 6:11).

"Temptation is the common experience of the people of God. We will never escape it as long as we live in a fallen world. But God has given us everything we need to win the battle." [54]

Taking God's Word to Heart

1. What compromises do we make that increase our vulnerability to temptation?

2. What lessons do we learn about Satan from his temptation of Jesus? What lessons do we learn from Jesus about how to withstand or overcome temptation?

3. How can we prepare for temptation before it comes? Give an example.

4. What do you need to do to have victory over a specific temptation in your life?

THESE THINGS I KNOW TO BE TRUE

Deuteronomy 33:27 (NIV)—*"The eternal God is your refuge, and underneath are the everlasting arms."*

Psalm 19:8—*The precepts of the LORD are right, rejoicing the heart; the commandment of the LORD is pure, enlightening the eyes.*

Romans 15:13—*May the God of hope fill you with all joy and peace in believing, so that by the power of the Holy Spirit you may abound in hope.*

Several years ago, while vacationing with my family at the summer home of some dear friends, the host asked me to give a devotional on what I would tell my children as my parting words in this life.

I wanted to say something profound, succinct, easy to remember, and helpful. As I pondered this request, five points came to me:

1. Trust God's Word above everything else.

2. Believe that God loves you.

3. Resist your enemy.

4. Be faithful in suffering.

5. Keep going—never give up.

I know that God's Word is true and trustworthy because He tells us that it is. With all the voices out there telling us to believe so many things that are not true, we need an anchor for our souls, a plumb line of truth that will never change. Many voices fill our ears and minds with falsehoods. We can't even trust our emotions because they change often—affected by our health, circumstances, other people, our spiritual condition, and the weather. We can experience fear, anger, depression, joy, peace, and a sense of well-being all in one day. God's Word exposes our innermost thoughts and desires (Hebrews 4:12). The Word of God is one of the few things that never changes.

We can't trust our circumstances because they can change from hour to hour—the economy, health, family relationships, accidents, disasters. Sometimes we can misinterpret our circumstances as being God's will when they are not. The prophet Jonah in his disobedience tried to run away from God. When he found a ship that was sailing in the opposite direction of where God had called him to go, he jumped aboard, thinking this circumstance meant he didn't have to obey God. We must be careful to never justify disobeying what we know God has called us to do based on Scripture.

I know that God loves us because His Word assures us in many places that He does. The Bible is filled with Scripture that teaches us about His love. Sometimes we think God doesn't love us or loves us less because we've done too many sinful things and failed Him in many ways. If God loved us enough to die for us, and we have accepted the Lord Jesus Christ as our Savior, nothing that we can ever do will separate us from His love or diminish His love for us.

We are assured of His love by these beautiful verses: "But God, being rich in mercy, because of the great love with which he loved us, even when we were dead in our trespasses, made us alive together with Christ—by grace you have been saved" (Ephesians 2:4-5).

I know that Satan is our enemy and that we are constantly in a spiritual warfare because His Word tells us he is. We are instructed how to behave in the fight against our enemy: "Submit yourselves therefore to God. Resist the devil, and he will flee from you. Draw near to God, and he will draw near to you" (James 4:7-8).

Satan will distort truth, deceive, and lie to us about many things.

His plan hasn't changed since the Garden of Eden when he lied to Adam and Eve about what God had said and deceived them into separation from their Creator's fellowship. Satan will try to destroy everything good in your life—marriage, children, grandchildren, character, relationships, jobs, finances. Study and memorize God's Word. Know your weaknesses. Put on the armor of God. Be sober-minded and watchful (1 Peter 5:8-9).

I know that I can be faithful in suffering because God's Word tells us that He will sustain us by His grace and give us peace in the midst of our trials. Again, Scripture instructs us how to behave when we are in painful and difficult circumstances: "Therefore let those who suffer according to God's will entrust their souls to a faithful Creator while doing good" (1 Peter 4:19). Tragedies, disasters, debilitating illnesses, and chronic pain will be part of our lives as long as we live on this earth. We are assured that in the midst of our suffering, God is refining and maturing us.

Finally, *I know that I can keep going and must never give up* because God's Word tells us we can: "Therefore, my dear brothers and sisters, stand firm. Let nothing move you. Always give yourselves fully to the work of the Lord, because you know that your labor in the Lord is not in vain" (1 Corinthians 15:58 NIV). If we sin or make a mistake, we can confess it, and ask God to forgive and cleanse us based on His promise in 1 John 1:9. Let's skip the pity parties and get back on track as quickly as possible.

When we're upset and don't get what we want, when we're discouraged or perplexed, instead of complaining, whining, getting angry, or saying hurtful things, we can accept them with grace and begin to give thanks. The veteran missionary to India Amy Carmichael, who suffered many difficulties, chronic pain, and illnesses, said, "In acceptance there is peace." By giving thanks, we honor God and remind ourselves that He is in charge and we can be faithful to the end. We can have joy on the journey. As Kay Warren reminds us, "Joy is the settled assurance that God is in control of all the details of my life, the quiet confidence that ultimately everything is going to be all right, and the determined choice to praise God in all things."

These things I know to be true!

Taking God's Word to Heart

1. How do you know without a doubt that "these things" are true?

2. When you are suffering, what does God's Word tell you to do?

3. Recall an experience when a specific truth in Scripture enabled you to go through a trial and kept you faithful.

4. Whenever a challenging or difficult circumstance enters your life, choose and memorize Scripture that will focus your attention away from your circumstance and back to God.

WISDOM

Proverbs 2:6-7, 10—*For the LORD gives wisdom;*
from his mouth come knowledge and understanding;
he stores up sound wisdom for the upright;
he is a shield to those who walk in integrity...
For wisdom will come into your heart,
and knowledge will be pleasant to your soul.

Proverbs 3:5-6—*Trust in the LORD with all your heart,*
and do not lean on your own understanding.
In all your ways acknowledge him,
and he will make straight your paths.

James 1:5-8 (NIV)—*If any of you lacks wisdom, you*
should ask God, who gives generously to all without finding
fault, and it will be given to you. But when you ask, you
must believe and not doubt, because the one who doubts
is like a wave of the sea, blown and tossed by the wind.

Life isn't a smooth highway. Potholes, speed bumps, and construction sites line the route. What we need is wisdom to sort out how we should respond to the detours, difficulties, and decisions we must make.

"I just don't know what to do!" We've all made that remark at some time in our lives. Parents say that when a teenager rebels; a couple states this when an elderly parent cannot live alone anymore; a young mother expresses that when her toddler throws tantrums or her third grader continues to struggle with reading; a husband voices it when he has been laid off his job; a distraught wife cries this when her husband asks for a divorce.

Wisdom is needed now more than ever because we live in perilous times. Job security is no more. Terror threats and wars abound. Families struggle to stay together. Immorality surrounds us. The availability of drugs threatens our young people. Natural disasters ravage our nation. We need wisdom to make the right choice in times of darkness and uncertainty.

Even normal decisions, such as what college to attend, which vocation to pursue, whom we should marry, how many children to have, where we should live, or where to invest our money, can demand wisdom beyond our understanding. Some decisions are forced upon us by people or circumstances beyond our control. Usually, it's easy to get the knowledge and facts we need and then list the pros and the cons. Human wisdom is the ability to apply knowledge, discernment, good judgment, and what we've learned from past experiences.

But wisdom is more than common sense. Making the right choice at a critical moment or in the midst of a trial requires divine help. Trials can bring us to our knees. God allows trials so that we might come to Him and develop those qualities of faith and endurance that He desires in our lives. Wisdom from God exceeds our human limitation of not knowing the future.

Did you know that wisdom is available? Every believer can receive it from God. As the verse quoted above reads, "If any of you lacks wisdom, you should ask God, who gives generously to all without finding fault, and it will be given to you. But when you ask, you must believe and not doubt, because the one who doubts is like a wave of the sea, blown and tossed by the wind" (James 1:5-6 NIV).

But how, specifically, do we receive this wisdom the Bible promises? James gives us three requirements for receiving special illumination from God to enable us to make wise decisions. I believe strongly that if we meet these requirements, God will answer. On the basis of God's promise and our obedience, we are assured that when we ask for wisdom, it will be given to us.

What are these requirements? *First, we must believe that God "gives generously to all without finding fault"* (1:5). James pictures God with His hand outstretched, waiting to give generously to those who ask. Believing this is not as easy as it may seem. Often we think that God is not generous. After all, if He were so concerned about us, we would expect Him to deliver us from our trials.

We are constantly in danger of building our theology on circumstances. We think that God's care for us means that we should never have cancer, be laid off from our job, have a rebellious child, or have a car accident. But in reality, God's love is seen within the context of such trials, and we must remember that He loves us regardless of the circumstances.

The Bible teaches us that God is compassionate, filled with loving kindness and tender emotion. In the Old Testament, God said that the one who touches Israel touches the apple of His eye. Of course, God has the same sensitivity toward His people today, and He is vitally interested in our lives. It is because God is merciful and delights in giving that He never reprimands those who come to Him. He never chides us by becoming upset when we come to Him repeatedly. Do you believe God is generous? Do you believe He cares about you? If so, you've met the first requirement to receive the special gift of wisdom.

Second, when we ask for wisdom, *we must "believe and not doubt"* (1:6) based on the promise of God's generosity. If God is generous, and yet we come to Him with doubts whether He will give us wisdom, we cannot expect an answer from Him. Obviously, if He desires to give and we meet the requirements, we can know for sure that He will give us the needed wisdom we are asking for.

Now James doesn't say that we will have our answer immediately. Many years ago my husband and I faced a crucial decision. He was asked to become the pastor of a church where he had been doing some interim preaching. We knew this decision would affect our lives for many years to come. We discussed the pros and cons, we weighed all the factors, but we simply did not know God's will. Finally, in desperation, we knelt together to claim James 1:5, and we asked in faith believing that God could and would give us wisdom. Then we drove to one of the elders' homes where we had to give an answer that evening.

As my husband met with the leaders of the church, he realized that God's will was for him to accept the call to pastor the church. That night we learned that God often does not give us the answer in advance. But when the deadline arrives, when we come to a fork in the road and must choose, God gives us wisdom in that moment to know what to do.

The *third* requirement is perhaps the most difficult. *We must truly believe God's Word and His promise* to give us wisdom. Let's look at the text again: "But when you ask, *you must believe and not doubt*, because the one who doubts is like a wave of the sea, blown and tossed by the wind" (1:6).

This means that we will have a single mind toward God. Then James adds, "That person should not expect to receive anything from the Lord. Such a person is double-minded and unstable in all they do" (1:7-8). That word *double-minded* literally means "two-souled." Double-mindedness means that one part of us wants God's will and another part wants our own will.

We've all done that. We come to God, hoping He will confirm the decision *we* want to make. We want His stamp of approval on the choice we've already made. But if we ask God for wisdom without being willing to surrender ourselves fully to His will, we are double-minded.

Are you feeling confused and perplexed? You may not know if you should marry that special person you have come to love, sell your house, send your child to public school or home school, go back to work to ease the financial strain, or take on the challenge of caring for an elderly parent. I believe that if you meet the requirements—believe that God is generous, ask in faith, have a single mind toward God— He is obligated to give you wisdom and prevent you from making a wrong choice.

A guideline to follow when making a decision is to never violate one of God's commands. If you want God to give you wisdom in facing the hard decisions of life, you must come with a complete willingness to do the will of God. Always obey His revealed will, and He will be faithful to give you wisdom for His unrevealed will.

How does God give this wisdom? Sometimes He gives insight through other people who are able to provide a different perspective on our problem. A word of caution: Do not brush aside warnings from others or ignore red flags. These are often the means God uses to reveal the wisdom you have asked for. At other times we receive insight through meditation on the Scriptures and through our obedience to what God has revealed. Finally, we have a sense or an intuition that we have discerned the mind of God. Nearly always we will have peace in our hearts that God is leading us to make a certain decision. Be very cautious to proceed until you have the peace of God, as He is usually not in a hurry to reveal His will.

However, you may approach the deadline and sense you do not have God's wisdom and peace yet. What do you do? Based on all your information, your obedience, and common sense, you make the best decision possible. If it is the wrong one, God is faithful to either stop you in some way or give you the grace and ability to live with it.

Finally, God does not give the gift of wisdom to everyone. That is not a contradiction. When James says, "If *any of you* lacks wisdom…" he is referring to fellow believers. Wisdom is given to those who believe that Jesus Christ's death on the cross will forgive and cleanse their sins. Paul says that Christ "became to us wisdom from God" (1 Corinthians 1:30). Wisdom is one of the many blessings that become ours when we accept the Lord Jesus Christ as our Savior. You can make that decision right now. Christ is waiting for you to say yes to Him so that you too can receive the wisdom and insight you need to make wise choices in life.

Aren't you glad God is generous? You can come to Him in faith, completely willing to do His will, and receive the wisdom and discernment you need to face the future. As Jesus said, "Ask, and it will be given to you; seek, and you will find; knock, and it will be opened to you" (Matthew 7:7).

Taking God's Word to Heart

1. It is possible to be smart but not wise. What is the difference between wisdom and knowledge, and how are they related to each other?

2. Using the truth of James 1, list the process by which we can receive divine wisdom. Evaluate past experiences when you sought wisdom from God.

3. What difficult decision are you facing today that you need wisdom for? With an undivided heart, ask God for the wisdom He promises in the way He has prescribed.

THE WORD OF GOD

2 Timothy 3:16—*All Scripture is breathed out by God and profitable for teaching, for reproof, for correction, and for training in righteousness.*

Hebrews 4:12—*For the word of God is living and active, sharper than any two-edged sword, piercing to the division of soul and of spirit, of joints and of marrow, and discerning the thoughts and intentions of the heart.*

Psalm 1:1-2 (NIV)—*Blessed is the one who does not walk in step with the wicked or stand in the way that sinners take or sit in the company of mockers, but whose delight is in the law of the LORD, and who meditates on his law day and night.*

Psalm 119:11—*I have stored up your word in my heart, that I might not sin against you.*

Many people hesitate to read the Bible because they think they won't be able to understand it. Or if they did understand it, they think it will be too hard to do what it says.

In Psalm 19 the Word of God promises to do remarkable things for us: breathe life into our souls, make us wise, bring joy to our hearts, give us discernment, warn us of error, and reward us if we obey it. We are wrong to think that the Bible is too complicated to understand unless we have a degree in theology or that we wouldn't be able to obey God's rules.

The Bible is a remarkable book with dual authorship; that is, it was written by men whose styles and backgrounds were different, and it was inspired by God the Holy Spirit—breathed out by God—in such a way that the original documents were kept from error (2 Timothy 3:16). When we hold a Bible, we are holding the Word of God. This same Spirit of God is present when we read it, and He helps us to comprehend it and make it relevant in our lives. It is the only book where the author is present every time you read it.

God's Word tells us many things that we wouldn't know if we did not have it, and it is the only written revelation that He has given to us. It is His love letter telling us who He is, the amazing things He has done since He created the universe (including the earth, the animals, and the first human beings), and how much He loves us. It is God's instruction manual telling us that we are sinners (and why), about His plan of redemption to send His Son to the earth to die on the cross for our sins, and how He wants us to live so that we can please Him. If we do not respect the Bible, then, most likely, we do not respect God.

The strongest, most accurate, and most descriptive statement about the Bible's power is found in Hebrews 4:12: "For the word of God is living and active, sharper than any two-edged sword, piercing to the division of soul and of spirit, of joints and of marrow, and discerning the thoughts and intentions of the heart." These words should not frighten us away from reading and studying the Bible, but draw us to it. It reveals that God knows us better than any other person does or that we can even know ourselves. God's Word reveals who we really are, and then teaches us how we can be truly happy by knowing and obeying God's instructions.

What does it mean that the Word of God is "living and active"? The Bible isn't just an ordinary book on a library shelf; it is alive with the authority of God Himself through His Spirit—filled with life and power. It is "the living and abiding word of God" (1 Peter 1:23). The phenomenon of Jesus Christ being the living Word is explained in John 1:1,14: "In the beginning was the Word, and the Word was with

God, and the Word was God…And the Word became flesh and dwelt among us, and we have seen his glory, glory as of the only Son from the Father, full of grace and truth." So it follows that the more we read and know the Word of God, the better we will know our Savior, the Living Word.

We should not be surprised that God's Word is compared to a sword. The ancient Roman soldier's sword had two edges so that it could cut both ways. The Word of God is "sharper than any double-edged sword"—it can dissect us and help us discern who we truly are and what we must do to establish a relationship with God. It wounds us so that it might heal us. [55] It penetrates to the innermost recesses of our spiritual being just as a scalpel cuts through the joints and down to the depths of the marrow of the bone where blood is manufactured—the life of the body. It stops at nothing until it comes to reality.

The Word of God also judges the thoughts and intentions of the heart. Greek scholar Kenneth Wuest says this means that our thoughts and motives are "sifted and analyzed" as evidence either for or against us. [56] Even our attitudes are examined by the holy Word of God—those thoughts that drive our motives and actions, what we believe. That's who we really are. This passage continues on to tell us that "no creature is hidden from his sight, but all are naked and exposed to the eyes of him to whom we must give account" (Hebrews 4:13). We move from the scrutiny of the written Word to the X-ray of the living Word, Jesus Christ. Nothing escapes His inspection; our entire body, soul, and spirit is cut apart and carefully examined for spiritual tumors, a diseased heart, or a hairline fracture of the soul.

I was an operating room nurse for several years and scrubbed for many surgeries. The patient was gently positioned, carefully anesthetized, and appropriately prepped and draped. Upon hearing the command "scalpel," I handed the knife to the surgeon, who cut through healthy, beautiful flesh down to where the tumor or diseased organ was. The healthy tissue had to be injured and traumatized in order to reach and remove the unhealthy tissue.

So it is with spiritual surgery. The cut of God's divine scalpel can be excruciating. But the Word of God is both the surgeon and the anesthesia. Grace is our pain medication and antibiotic as we go through the healing process. We are wounded so that we may be healed and brought to a state of spiritual health. Psalm 147:3 comforts us with these words,

> He heals the brokenhearted
>   and binds up their wounds.

The Word of God equips us to *obey* the Word of God. That's why studying the Bible, memorizing it, and meditating on it are so important.

God spoke the following words to Joshua as Moses's successor to lead the Israelites into the land He was giving them,

> "This Book of the Law shall not depart from your mouth,
> but you shall meditate on it day and night, so that you may
> be careful to do according to all that is written in it. For
> then you will make your way prosperous, and then you will
> have good success" (Joshua 1:8).

God's Word is preparing us for something. We don't need to know what it is, but we know that we must be ready—to suffer, defeat the devil, minister to others, share the gospel, fail, succeed, and perhaps someday, be a martyr defending our faith.

In his book *Passages: How Reading the Bible in a Year Will Change Everything for You,* Brian Hardin tells us how the Word of God changed his life, and how it will change ours:

> I've read through the Bible in large portions seven days a
> week for well over two thousand days consecutively. The
> man that I was is no longer here. I don't look at the world
> the same in any way. I liken this to working out at the
> gym. If you stick with it a month, you begin to feel healthy.

Sweat it out for a quarter of a year and new lines of lean muscle begin to appear. Hang with it for a year and you'll have a new body and the energy to go along with it. Our hearts seem to work the same way. I'm inviting you to the adventure, and I am quite certain that if you expose yourself to the Scriptures every day for a while, there is no way for you to remain the same.

If you will commit yourself to spending every day in the Bible for one month, you will notice something shifting inside. If you'll do it for three months, you'll feel as if major places in your heart are coming back to life. If you'll stick to it for a year, you will be transformed from the inside out. [57]

That's the Word of God: Convicts. Converts. Cleanses. Counsels. Comforts. Constrains.

Do you love your Bible? Is it precious to you? Does it give you strength to face each day no matter what is going on in your life? I have been reading out of the very same Bible for the past twenty-three years—every book, every page is marked with red pencil. I consider it my most valuable possession, precious and beloved. It is a treasure of truth, a haven of hope, a cup of comfort, a gift of grace, a place of peace, a shelter of strength, a potpourri of promises, a refuge of righteousness, and the limitless love of God—everything I need to become a woman of God.

Nancy Leigh DeMoss is a godly woman who has influenced thousands of women to walk in the freedom and fullness of Christ through the ministry of Revive Our Hearts. She has said, "I'm convinced that no personal discipline will do more than consistent time in God's Word to help you know God, walk in His ways, and experience the reality of His grace in your life."

Taking God's Word to Heart

1. What barriers often keep us from consistently reading God's

Word, and how can we overcome them? Ask God to give you a deep love for His Word.

2. List some of the promises in the Bible to those who "meditate" on it. Why is the Word of God so powerful?

3. Choose to consistently spend time reading and studying the Bible. Begin to meditate on the Word by choosing a passage such as Romans 8 and ask these questions: What do these verses teach me about God? Do they have a promise for me? What do they ask me to do?

WORRY 58

Matthew 6:31-34 (NIV)—*"So do not worry, saying, 'What shall we eat?' or 'What shall we drink?' or 'What shall we wear?' For the pagans run after all these things, and your heavenly Father knows that you need them. But seek first his kingdom and his righteousness, and all these things will be given to you as well. Therefore do not worry about tomorrow, for tomorrow will worry about itself. Each day has enough trouble of its own."*

Philippians 4:6-7—*Do not be anxious about anything, but in everything by prayer and supplication with thanksgiving let your requests be made known to God. And the peace of God, which surpasses all understanding, will guard your hearts and your minds in Christ Jesus.*

1 Peter 5:7—*Casting all your anxieties on him, because he cares for you.*

Worry is mental or emotional distress resulting from concern about a difficulty or problem, which may produce a negative response in our behavior or emotions. We may experience a cascade of reactions: anxiety, fear, apprehension, uneasiness, stress, despair, depression. Worry gives too much power to our emotions, even though we can't trust our feelings.

What happens when we worry? We become distracted, preoccupied, sapped of energy, and robbed of joy, peace, time, sleep, and productivity. Corrie ten Boom said, "Worry does not empty tomorrow of

185

its sorrow, it empties today of its strength." Worry is an indication that we are trying to solve our problems on our own.

Why do we worry? We believe that things are out of control and that no one is in charge. We have a need and don't know how to meet it. We have a problem and don't know how to fix it. We have a crisis and don't know how to handle it. We want a situation to turn out a certain way, so we try to manipulate circumstances and people.

Francis Chan said that, "Worry implies that we don't quite trust that God is big enough, powerful enough, or loving enough to take care of what's happening in our lives."

Worry also means "to be torn in two." And that is exactly what anxiety does—it tears us apart. Worry is like putting on the brakes and stepping on the gas at the same time. Our bodies might obediently go in one direction, but our minds are somewhere else. We live with tension and can't enjoy the present moment. Worry causes us to work against ourselves and hinders our fellowship with God.

I read the account of a psychologist teaching a class on stress management. She held up a glass of water and asked, "How heavy is this glass of water?" The answers ranged from eight ounces to twenty ounces. She replied,

> The absolute weight doesn't matter. It depends on how long I hold it. If I hold it for a minute, it's not a problem. If I hold it for an hour, I'll have an ache in my arm. If I hold it for a day, my arm will feel numb and paralyzed. In each case, the weight of the glass doesn't change, but the longer I hold it, the heavier it becomes.
>
> The stresses and worries in life are like that glass of water. Think about them for a while and nothing happens. Think about them a bit longer and they begin to hurt. And if you think about them all day long, you will feel paralyzed—incapable of doing anything. Remember to put the glass down.

When speaking to His disciples, Jesus gave three reasons why we *should not* worry, and then three reasons why we *don't have to* worry.

First, He says we should not worry because of who we are. "Look at the birds of the air; they do not sow or reap or store away in barns, and yet your heavenly Father feeds them. Are you not much more valuable than they?" (Matthew 6:26). Jesus is saying that when we worry, we diminish our value.

Second, we should not worry because it is useless. "Can any one of you by worrying add a single hour to your life?" (6:27). Worry might be worth it if it added to the length of our life; but in fact, it might diminish it. Worry will not change anything. Our anxious thoughts and feelings will not make a problem go away.

Third, we should not worry because of our testimony. "For the pagans run after all these things, and your heavenly Father knows that you need them" (6:32). When we worry we act like the heathen who do not know the heavenly Father. Two people get cancer, one is a Christian, the other is not. How tragic if the Christian accepts it no better than the unbeliever.

But how do we overcome worry or anxiety? Three words in this narrative will help us.

First is the word *Father*. We find it more difficult to trust our heavenly Father than our earthly father because our heavenly Father is less predictable. Our earthly father would prevent us from having accidents and spare us the pain and suffering from cancer if it were within his power to do so. That doesn't mean our heavenly Father loves us less; He loves us with a perfect love. But He is willing to allow us to experience loss and pain for a greater, eternal good. God wants to accomplish things in our lives that only pain, suffering, and difficulties can bring about.

The second word is *faith*. "You of little *faith*," Jesus said (6:30). Most of us have weak faith and God wants to develop it so that we will trust Him and have confidence in His sovereignty. Our faith grows when it is exercised, and trials give it great opportunities to grow. Faith is built through an understanding of God's promises.

Finally, the last word is *first*. "But seek *first* his kingdom and his righteousness, and all these things will be given to you as well" (6:33). We get so busy worrying about how our needs will be met or how things will turn out that we forget to seek God's kingdom and righteousness. Our worries show that we consider our needs and problems more important than seeking and knowing God. But we have it all backward. If we seek Him first and choose to obey His commands, *then* He will give us what we need.

What happens when we don't worry? We're relieved of our burden, our joy returns, we have more time and energy, and our faith grows. It frees us to see and imagine what God may and will do to solve our problems and meet our needs. When we don't know what to do, we take the next logical step.

Henry Blackaby says that God is always working even when we can't see anything happening. "He will surprise you by working out things in a better way, a different way, a God way—if you let Him!"

God sends difficult situations and people into our lives to test us and cause our faith to grow. There are no easy answers to many painful situations, yet we must be convinced that these matters are in God's hands and that God is good. It has been said that *what God does in us while we wait is more important than what we wait for.*

Some people pray and pray but are never free of anxiety. What's wrong? Perhaps their prayers are just a rehearsal of their problems and burdens as they beg and plead with God. However, it insults God when we constantly bombard Him with our worries.

Through prayer, we must consciously surrender and give our anxieties and problems to the Lord. Imagine yourself casting your cares upon Jesus (1 Peter 5:7). This doesn't mean you will never have another worry or never feel sorrow and grief; it does mean you have confidence that God knows what you are going through and is working these things together for good according to His purposes. Allow the peace of God to *guard* your mind and heart from anxious thoughts (Philippians 4:7).

If the anxiety returns, it may be an attack of Satan. Following the verse to cast our cares on Jesus is a warning to be sober-minded and watchful because our adversary the devil is prowling around like a lion looking for someone to devour. We are commanded to resist him, remaining firm in our faith, knowing that our brothers and sisters throughout the world are experiencing the same kinds of suffering (1 Peter 5:8-9).

We resist the devil in the name of Jesus, and we break his power to keep us bound in our anxieties by affirming our faith and position in Christ, saved and covered by His blood. We then reaffirm our decision to leave our worries with God, rejecting any thoughts of them.

God does not leave us without encouragement and hope. The next verse gives us perspective as to what God is doing through the burdens and trials we have cast upon Him. "And after you have suffered a little while, the God of all grace, who has called you to his eternal glory in Christ, will himself restore, confirm, strengthen, and establish you" (1 Peter 5:10).

I love this promise. It tells me that the *God of all grace* is working through my sufferings to repair, prove, fortify, and authenticate me as His child…for His glory.

> But he knows the way that I take;
>   when he has tried me, I shall come out as gold.
>   (Job 23:10)

Some time ago my then nine-year-old granddaughter, Abigail, was worried about doing a project at school the next day. Before praying for her I said, "Abby, did you know there's a verse in the Bible that talks about worry?" Turning to Matthew 6:34, I asked her to read it aloud: "Therefore do not worry about tomorrow, for tomorrow will worry about itself. Each day has enough trouble of its own" (NIV).

Her eyes got big and a smile lit her face as she said, "Mimi, I don't have to worry because Jesus already knows about tomorrow!"

Taking God's Word to Heart

1. What do you worry about the most? Why is it sinful and useless to worry?

2. What does worry do to us emotionally, spiritually, and physically?

3. How are we able to give our worries to God and trust Him to take care of us?

WOUNDEDNESS AND HEALING

Psalm 147:3—*He heals the brokenhearted
and binds up their wounds.*

Ephesians 4:29-30—*Let no corrupting talk come out of
your mouths, but only such as is good for building up, as
fits the occasion, that it may give grace to those who hear.*

1 Peter 4:18—*Therefore let those who suffer
according to God's will entrust their souls to
a faithful Creator while doing good.*

Our past can have great power over us, especially if we are defined by the wounds of our past. This chapter is a message of hope, not as an answer to all of our struggles, but as a ladder to help us begin the journey out of the pit to be set free from the prison of guilt, fear, bitterness, anger, self-loathing, and hatred.

Some of our wounds are caused by others' sin against us but also by our own sin. Other wounds come from the tragic events of life, such as devastating accidents, the death of a loved one, a chronic illness, a sexual assault, loss of a good job or a forced career change, a rebellious child, divorce, rejection, and betrayal. Then there are the acts of God that bring devastation to many: tornados, earthquakes, tsunamis, fires, and floods.

However, I think the deepest wounds are caused within the walls of our homes from such things as alcoholism, divorce, and abuse. There are wounds from parents who were absent, neglectful, and verbally, physically, or sexually abusive. A wounded heart can be the first step on the path toward a rebellious and bitter heart, as it says in Proverbs 14:10:

> The heart knows its own bitterness,
> and no stranger shares its joy.

It can lead us to justify our own sin and treat others the way we were treated. Those who marry often do so with the expectation that their mate will heal them and make them happy. But that's like asking your partner to fill in the Grand Canyon with a shovel. People expect marriage to do for them what only God can do. Wives, especially, use the power of their wounds to control their husbands.

Wounded people often hold hurt and anger inside, thinking it will give them power to control people and situations. But it is a deceptive power because the ones they hurt the most are themselves. Woundedness becomes a prison, a kind of safe place where no one dares to hurt them again or challenge their pain. They think their dysfunctional life and problems have been caused by their parents, mate, boyfriend or girlfriend, boss, or someone who abused or betrayed them. They play the blame game—their own sin is justified by thinking that someone else is responsible. Victims often make other victims…of their pain, hurt, anger, control. Hurting people hurt other people.

Wounded people pass through life repeating these questions:

"Why did this happen to me?"

"Why don't you feel sorry for me?"

"Why am I empty, lonely, and in pain?"

"If you care about me, why don't you heal my wound?"

It has been said that "woundology" is the practice of keeping death near you. Some people fear healing because they would have to take personal responsibility for their lives. They think that others might take advantage of them and, more to the point, that the person who caused their wound might get away with what they've done and never be brought to justice. Their wounds give them permission to be just who they are. They talk and act as if they are the only person who has ever been victimized. As Michael Easley said, "If you are defined by your struggles, you will be a victim. If you are defined by your identity in Christ, you will be a fellow-sufferer."

Dr. Kevin Elko analyzed it this way, "The fact of the matter is we all suffer. It did not happen specifically just to you and me. It has happened to the world. One of the reasons that we get so caught up in the 'whys' is we believe that we were the only ones hurt. That is not true. If we all told our stories we would find the entire world has been wounded." [59]

Here are some steps that can help the wounded on their journey to wholeness.

First, we must take responsibility for the sinful attitudes that we have allowed to control us. Wounded people are often so consumed by the sins of others that they cannot see their own. Having been sinned against, the great temptation of the wounded person is to sin against others. They will never see their own reactions as sinful unless someone points it out, or they are desperate enough to ask God to reveal it to them. If we have wounds, we must recognize and face our pain honestly and stop inflicting it on others. In short, we must own our own stuff.

Here are some questions that will help us face our pain in a beneficial way:

- "What can I learn from what happened to me?"
- "How can I get to a place of healing and wholeness?"
- "How can God make my pain and woundedness 'work together for good' to bring glory to Himself?"

Second, we have to confess our own sin that God has shown us and allow Him to forgive and cleanse us: "If we confess our sins, he is faithful and just to forgive us our sins and to cleanse us from all unrighteousness" (1 John 1:9). In the process, tell God exactly how you feel and how much you hurt. Give Him your pain, anger, and bitterness. As Betsie ten Boom said, "There is no pit so deep but that God is not deeper still." Our sin is covered—put away forever.

The third step in healing is clearing our consciences. First Timothy 1:5 says, "The aim of our charge is love that issues from a pure heart and a good conscience and a sincere faith." Some of us will never form harmonious relationships until our conscience is cleared, not just before God, but before others. We must confess to others our anger, our desire to control them, our false accusations, and our excuses for blaming others for our lot in life.

The fourth step is to forgive as we have been forgiven. It is being willing to part with our bitterness and anger: "Be kind to one another, tenderhearted, forgiving one another, as God in Christ forgave you" (Ephesians 4:32). God's forgiveness is our example as to how to forgive others. Our heavenly Father, knowing ahead of time what awful sinners we would become, sent Jesus to die in our place to bear our sin and pain.

How do we in turn forgive others? It is an act of the will even though it involves our emotions; it is a choice. If Jesus can forgive you, then you can forgive yourself. If Jesus can forgive others, so can you. We cannot take justice into our own hands. That belongs to God.

Forgiveness does not minimize the evil and horror of what happened to us, nor does it allow our victimizer off the hook. But the benefit of forgiveness will be much greater for us as we are released from the prison of pain we have been living in. It is said that bitterness is like drinking poison and expecting someone else to die. Our wounds can destroy us, not the person who inflicted them upon us.

If you are still holding onto a perception, a memory, that something was done to you that has affected your whole life, you must now see your pain and loss as an event that must be put under the blood of Christ, looked at and nursed no more. Years ago I heard a counselor say, "Walk through every memory and cut the rope and let them go. Listen to your hurt, limit yourself as you grieve your loss, and then let it go." You may even choose to have a trusted friend or relative sit with you to witness the grieving over your wounds and verify that you are done with it. You are then free to give yourself to Jesus and let Him take back the power and control of your life.

Fifth, and this is critical, *we must renew our mind with Scripture* and grasp the wonderful reality that our identity is not that of a victim but of a daughter of God, welcomed by God as a part of His family. In Christ, we are a "new creation" (2 Corinthians 5:17), which gives us the ability to view life from a new perspective.

Healing is a process. Don't be discouraged if your process of healing is slow. You might have to repeat the steps in this brief chapter many times. Now, you can *give your wounds to Jesus* once for all. Don't keep peeling back the scab to see if healing has occurred. Begin to see yourself through His wounds and not your own.

> But he was pierced for our transgressions;
>> he was crushed for our iniquities;
> upon him was the chastisement that brought us peace,
>> and with his wounds we are healed.
>> (Isaiah 53:5)

Meditate on what God has done for you, not on what someone else did to you long ago.

Finally, speak with hope and expectation rather than despair. With renewed dependence on Christ, let your vocabulary change. Begin talking about what you are learning from your Bible study, give praise to the Lord, thank God for preserving you through all of your trials. Believe His Word: "He heals the broken hearted and binds up their wounds" (Psalm 147:3).

God recycles our past. He turns our wounds into scars. Scars are an indication that a wound has healed. Jesus's scars show us that the work of the cross is finished. Our scars will be a trophy to His finished work of forgiveness, grace, and healing. Romans 8:28 tells us that God can make all things—even evil—work together for good for those who love Him.

Let God redeem your story for His glory and for your peace of soul.

Think of how wonderful and good it is to be free and well. With God's leading, chart a new course for your future. Take your Savior's hand and let Him walk through the darkness with you out into the light and hope of a new day. May these words from Nancy Leigh DeMoss give you strength: "God wants you to run to Him in the midst of your pain—to give you the grace to be set free from any bondage to that hurt." [60]

Taking God's Word to Heart

1. Why do some people prefer woundedness over healing?

2. Ask yourself, "Am I ready to acknowledge my wounds and take ownership of them? Am I desperate enough to allow God to heal my wounds?"

3. Are you willing to do whatever God reveals for you to do? What might He ask you to do?

NOTES

1. Diane Hawkins, *How Protected Are You? The Christian's Spiritual Armor* (Grottoes, VA: Restoration in Christ Ministries, 2009), 25.

2. I am indebted to the booklet *Coming to Grips with God's Discipline of the Believer* by Erwin W. Lutzer (Chicago: Moody Press, 1991) for some of the insights presented in this chapter.

3. Doug Helmer, "Correcting Work of God," sermon on March 7, 2010, Harvest Bible Chapel, Avon, Indiana.

4. Nancy Leigh DeMoss, *The Quiet Place: Daily Devotional Readings* (Chicago: Moody Publishers, 2012), August 1.

5. Helmer, "Correcting Work of God."

6. Ibid.

7. Erwin Lutzer, "A Faith that Endures," sermon preached at Moody Church, September 1, 2013. Also, Ray Pritchard's ministry Keep Believing (www.keepbelieving.com) encourages people to do just that through real-life stories and sermons.

8. Dietrich Bonhoeffer, from "Sermon on Revelation 3:20, Barcelona, First Sunday in Advent, December 2, 1928," trans. Douglas W. Stott, ed. Clifford J. Green (Minneapolis: Fortress Press, 2008), 544-46.

9. Larry Renetzky, *Significant Living Magazine*, n.d., 40.

10. Robertson McQuilkin, *Moody Monthly*, November 1994, 17.

11. William H. Walton, quoted by Shirley Rose in "Finding Forgiveness," *Significant Living Magazine*, n.d., 13.

12. Renetzky.

13. Kay Arthur, Christmas letter, n.d.

14. Tina Stalker, "Focus on Forgiveness," *Christian Working Woman Newsletter*, n.d.

15. Kay Arthur, quoted by Rose in "Finding Forgiveness," 13.

16. McQuilkin.

17. Ellen Michaud, "Learning to Forgive," Rodale Press, December 18, 1998.

18. Kevin Elko, *Coping Magazine*, November/December 1994, 35.

19. My story presented here is expanded from what I wrote for *Jesus, Lover of a Woman's Soul* (Carol Stream, IL: Tyndale House Publishers, 2006), 115-18.

20. Sue Edwards, "The Cleavage Gap," *FullFill* (blog), March 19, 2012.

21. Rebecca Konyndyk DeYoung, *Glittering Vices* (Grand Rapids: Brazos Press, 2009), 163; quoted in Rosalie de Rosset, *Unseduced and Unshaken* (Chicago: Moody Publishers, 2012), 195.

22. Edwards, "Cleavage Gap."

23. Stacie Parlee-Johnson, "A Theology of Modesty: Naked Yet Unashamed," in Rosalie de Rosset, *Unseduced and Unshaken* (Chicago: Moody Publishers, 2012), 189.

24. Ibid.

25. Ibid., 192.

26. Ibid., 193.

27. Ibid.

28. Ibid., 194.

29. Ibid., 185.

30. Ibid., page 197.

31. Hana Yasmeen Ali, "You're Far More Precious," *Idealmuslimah*, http://idealmuslimah.com/dress/ hijaab/220-youre-far-more-precious.

32. Shara McKee, quoted in Fallon Erickson, "Royal Call to Resurrect Modesty!" *Girls Becoming* (blog), November 15, 2012, http://girlsbecoming.blogspot.com/2012_11_01_archive.html.

33. Stephen Davey, "Why Pray?" *Wisdom for the Heart* (blog), August 12, 2013, www.wisdomonline .org/devotionals/devotion_detail.html?id=276.

34. Jill Briscoe, *Renewal on the Run: Encouragement for Wives Who Are Partners in Ministry* (Wheaton, IL: Harold Shaw Publishers, 1992), reprinted in *Just Between Us* magazine, Fall 1994.

35. Ibid.

36. Quoted in Davey, "Why Pray?"

37. *Our Daily Bread*, December 29, 1993.

38. Erwin and Rebecca Lutzer, *Jesus, Lover of a Woman's Soul* (Carol Stream, IL: Tyndale House Publishers, 2006), 53.

39. Ibid., 53-54.

40. Ibid., 57.

41. John Piper, "Seven Things to Pray for Your Children," *Desiring God* (blog), July 13, 2013, www .desiringgod.org/blog/posts/seven-things-to-pray-for-your-children.

42. Ibid.

43. Cyndy Shearer, "All Prodigals Here," *Home Educating Family*, 2013 Issue 1, 28.

44. Ibid., 30.

45. Nancy Leigh DeMoss, *The Quiet Place: Daily Devotional Readings* (Chicago: Moody Publishers, 2012), "The Son of Tears," May 22.

46. Donor letter, Alliance Defending Freedom, August 2013.

47. I am indebted to the book *Why Good People Do Bad Things* by Erwin W. Lutzer for some of the insights in this chapter.

48. Rodney Clapp, "Shame Crucified," *Christianity Today*, 11 March 1991, 28, quoted by Erwin Lutzer, *Why Good People Do Bad Things* (Nashville, TN: W Publishing Group, 2001), 77.

49. Ibid., 78.

50. Ibid.

51. ESV Online Study Bible, Matthew 4:1-11, "Temptations of the Messiah."

52. Erwin W. Lutzer, "What Satan Wants," *Moody Monthly*, March/April, 1998, 27.

53. Ibid., 28.

54. Ray Pritchard, "From Temptation to Triumph," *Moody Monthly*, March/April, 1998, 23.

55. Erwin and Rebecca Lutzer, *Life-Changing Bible Verses You Should Know* (Eugene, OR: Harvest House Publishers, 2011), 169.

56. Ibid., 170.

57. Brian Hardin, *Passages: How Reading the Bible in a Year Will Change Everything for You* (Grand Rapids, MI: Zondervan, 2011), excerpted in *Significant Living*, n.d., 29.

58. For some of the insights in this chapter, I am indebted to Warren Wiersbe for a sermon he preached on "Worry" at Moody Church in the seventies.

59. Kevin Elko, "Learning to Forgive," *Coping Magazine*, November/December 1994, 35.

60. Nancy Leigh DeMoss, *Revive Our Hearts,* www.ReviveOurHearts.com.

ACKNOWLEDGMENTS

Writing a book is a collaborative process. I want to thank Harvest House Publishers for their confidence that I had something important to say from God's Word to women today. I am grateful to my editor, Rod Morris, whose patience and expertise have helped to shape this book to ensure it makes sense, and is accurate and concise.

I especially want to thank my dear husband, Erwin Lutzer, whose support, encouragement, wisdom, and prayers kept me going. He generously supplied me with salient points and godly counsel, directed me to supporting resources, and checked my theology. Many of the truths he has preached over the years found their way into this book, enriching and enhancing its content.

I am so very thankful for my sweet daughters and many dear friends who prayed and believed in me as I wrote: Lorisa, Lynette, Lisa, Gabriella, Donna, Lois, Evelyn, Rosie, Carol, Beth, Mary, Julie, Kristi, Patti, Lynne, Debbie, Gwen, Nancy, Bobbi, Margaret, Joy, Barb, and Connie.

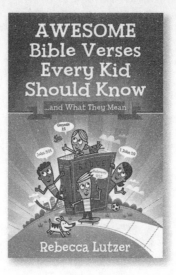

Awesome Bible Verses Every Kid Should Know
…and What They Mean

Now children ages 7 to 12 can enjoy the Bible's most important passages in a fun and engaging format. Youngsters will love this book's cartoon-like art, open layout, and kid-friendly language. Each two-page spread features…

- a verse set in an appealing "Bible" graphic
- a brief, accessible explanation and application of the passage
- open-ended questions adults can use to help kids talk about their faith

This easy-to-use tool will help parents, grandparents, Sunday school teachers, and other Christian workers sow the seeds of Scripture deeply into children's hearts.

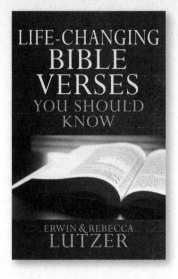

Life-Changing Bible Verses You Should Know

After Erwin Lutzer, senior pastor of the Moody Church, and his wife, Rebecca, realized that memorizing Scripture has nearly become a lost pursuit today, they decided to create this practical, relevant resource filled with powerful verses and insightful explanations to help stimulate a spiritual hunger in readers' lives. With more than 35 topics and questions for reflection and further study, readers will discover how God's Word will:

- sustain them in times of need
- comfort them in seasons of sorrow
- strengthen their hearts in times and areas of weakness
- direct their steps and decisions toward God's will

These handpicked verses provide a foundation of wisdom and hope to show readers who God is and what He has done for them, as well as who they are and how they can successfully live the Christian life.

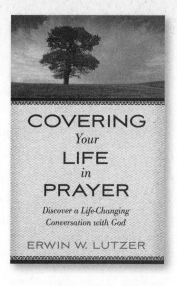

Covering Your Life in Prayer

Every Christian longs for a better and more intimate prayer life. And one of the most effective ways to grow more powerful in prayer is to learn from the prayers of others. In this way you will discover new ways to pray—new requests, concerns, and expressions of thanks you can bring to God's throne of grace. *Covering Your Life in Prayer* is an opportunity to listen in to a wide variety of personal and heartwarming prayers—prayers for…

- personal peace and faithfulness in difficult situations
- wisdom when making tough decisions
- a better understanding of your place in God's plans
- a willingness to cease struggling and let God be God
- God's work in the lives of both loved ones and unsaved friends

You will find this a wonderful resource for expanding your prayer horizons and enriching your relationship with God.

To learn more about Harvest House books and
to read sample chapters, visit our website:

www.harvesthousepublishers.com

HARVEST HOUSE PUBLISHERS
EUGENE, OREGON